NEW ⇒ WEST
C U I S I N E

NEW ⇒ WEST
C U I S I N E
FRESH RECIPES FROM THE ROCKY MOUNTAINS

Chase Reynolds Ewald and Amy Jo Sheppard

Photographs by Audrey Hall

Gibbs Smith, Publisher
TO ENRICH AND INSPIRE HUMANKIND
Salt Lake City | Charleston | Santa Fe | Santa Barbara

First Edition
12 11 10 09 08   5 4 3 2 1

Published by
Gibbs Smith, Publisher
P.O. Box 667
Layton, Utah 84041

Orders: 1.800.835.4993
www.gibbs-smith.com

Designed by Adrienne Pollard
Printed and bound in China

Library of Congress Cataloging-in-Publication Data
Ewald, Chase Reynolds, 1963-
   New West cuisine : fresh recipes from the Rocky Mountains / Chase Reynolds
Ewald and Amy Jo Sheppard ; photographs by Audrey Hall. — 1st ed.
      p. cm.
   Includes index.
   ISBN-13: 978-1-4236-0256-9
   ISBN-10: 1-4236-0256-0
   1. Cookery, American—Western style. 2. Cookery—West (U.S.)
3. Restaurants—West (U.S.)—Guidebooks. I. Sheppard, Amy Jo, 1965- II. Title.

TX715.2.W47E93 2008
641.5978—dc22
                              2007041120

For Addie, Jessie, Ross, and Katherine,

who make every meal an adventure

and an inspiration.

—CRE

To my family in Iowa,

who first brought me out West;

and to Clay, my family in the West today.

—AJS

CONTENTS ⫸

ACKNOWLEDGEMENTS

THIS BOOK, OF COURSE, would be nothing without the many talented chefs and artisans who opened their doors, their kitchens, and their recipe boxes to us in our pursuit of New West Cuisine. To all those featured in this book, we extend our heartfelt thanks. It has been a pleasure and a privilege to work with you—if, in fact, one can call it working at all!

Our editor, Lisa Anderson, deserves our eternal appreciation for her incredible attention to detail (leaving the spinach out of spinach soup would really not have gone over well). We are so grateful to Adrienne Pollard for her design expertise and artist's eye in helping make this book beautiful. Thanks, too, to our agent, Stephanie Cabot, whose professionalism allowed us to focus our creative energy on the fun stuff. Our photographer, Audrey Hall, created the most beautiful images, images that capture not only the delectability of the cuisine but the uniqueness and character of each wonderful restaurant, inn, or farm. Her warmth shines through in each photo.

And, finally, thanks to our sometimes neglected but always well-fed husbands, Clay Scott and Charles Ewald. Without you, there would be little reason to cook!

AMY JO grew up on a family farm along the Mississippi River in Iowa, where her dad and uncles raised beef and dairy cattle, corn, and soybeans, and ran a good old-fashioned Feed and Seed Store, the type that sold work boots, too. Those were the days when farms displayed the names of their farms on their silos—and not cute, catchy phrases, like Rising Sun Ranch or Green Acre Farms. They were proudly, and always, the eldest male's name "and Sons." Amy Jo's dad's farm was "H.J. Sheppard and Sons" (H.J. being her grandfather). Those days are long gone, with the sons of sons now working in Des Moines or Chicago, having traded tractors for keyboards and a house in the suburbs.

Amy Jo vividly remembers scouting trips to the Iowa stockyards with her dad, always followed up by a stop at the Stockyard Café for lunch or a piece of pie for her and coffee for her dad. In those days people could smoke indoors, and her dad favored King Edward cigars at that time. Amy Jo would listen to the (mostly) men discuss horseflesh and beef prices amid the smell of cigarette smoke, hot coffee, and frying bacon.

Today traditional cafés still exist in working stockyards, but working stockyards are fast becoming a thing of the past. Amy Jo's favorite Montana stockyard café is typical of stockyard cafés across the country: a small space dominated by a horseshoe-shaped counter with the kitchen in the middle and a few tables against the exterior wall. It is cluttered and chaotic, with cinnamon rolls cooling on top of the CD player, and a steaming berry crisp next to the cash register. The most photogenic thing in the place is the owner. She has a beautiful smile, which you're not guaranteed to see; she is all business.

The old-fashioned Stockyard Café is just one example of how—amid the processed cheese, frozen vegetable medley, and shipments from Sysco so ubiquitous not just in the Rockies but all over America—there are still culinary treasures to be discovered throughout the Mountain West. As William Least Heat Moon noted in his epic American travelogue *Blue Highways,* drivers should be on the lookout for the unassuming spot with a cluster of pickup trucks and police cars outside: that's where the stews are homemade

and the coffee is rich and hot. Truck stops along the lonely interstates of Nevada, Montana, Wyoming, and South Dakota involve running a gauntlet of neon beer advertisements, mass-processed beef jerky, muscle magazines, and slot machines to get to the real food. But truckers appreciate a good meal, and these places are often showcases for some anonymous country kitchen baker who has a light touch with baking powder biscuits and old-fashioned pie crusts—even if the fruit does come out of a number ten can. In the Mountain West, one should take culinary good intentions where one can find them.

The quirky and the unexpected are what make traveling the West's back roads so special. There is a hidden West behind the contemporary facade of Sinclair gas stations, Super Wal-Marts, and curio shops selling items mass made in China. There are all-you-can-eat pancake specials in West Yellowstone where the pancakes are the size of a dinner plate; traditional Basque restaurants in Elko, Nevada, where the food is served family-style on communal platters; famous malted milkshakes in the historic drugstore in tiny Dubois, Wyoming; and fried pickles at the Star Bakery in the antique mining town of Nevada City, Montana (first opened in 1865 to serve miners meals, beer, and fresh bread).

Nora's Fish Creek Inn in Wilson, Wyoming, with its gargantuan plastic trout on the roof, serves as the unofficial town hall for the tiny mountain-bound community; it's a place where billionaires tuck into their fried trout breakfast elbow-to-elbow at the counter with local plumbers, electricians, and hunting guides. Near the sophisticated university town of Bozeman, Montana, one of the best bets for steak is called The Land of Magic, and the fifty-three-mile round-trip drive through often dangerous conditions deters no one. At the steakhouse's annual "branding party" in May they shake off the winter doldrums with a huge outdoor steak fry; after some cold beer, local ranchers burn their brands into the restaurant's log walls. At Cassie's, in Cody, Wyoming, meat is not just cooked to order but cut to order; hungry patrons have been known after a successful elk hunt to order thirty-two-ounce prime ribs, the meat draped across the platter and hanging off either end. The Bear Creek Saloon, located on a lonely road near Red Lodge, Montana, in a former town done in by its underground coal mine disaster in the 1940s, staves off boredom and attracts customers with iguana races and a summertime "golf classic" amid the sagebrush, the Saloon owner officiating on horseback. And the food is good, too.

Sadly, good food is not ubiquitous in the West, and the treasures are often hidden. It's a challenge to prepare fresh, wholesome meals two hours from the nearest town in a time of high fuel costs and careful spenders, and in a climate with a short growing season and midsummer frosts. Chase, a non-meat-eater, recalls first coming to work on guest ranches in Wyoming at age eighteen. At that time, the bread was all white, the lettuce all iceberg, and the cheese always American. But there were high points, where old-fashioned chefs—though still relying heavily on the big truck deliveries of canned tomatoes and beans—did make their own salad dressings, prepared desserts from scratch, relied as much as possible on the ranch's high-country garden, and made sure the pastry chef was up at four every morning to begin the day's biscuits. But all too often the vegetables were precut and frozen, and certainly no one was talking about organic.

But times are changing, and new west cuisine reflects that. Today, not only are enlightened chefs producing fresh, creative meals in virtually every pocket of the Rocky Mountain West, but the idea of "organic," "local," and "sustainable" food is a household concept. Farmers' markets abound, despite the short growing season. Slow Food chapters, or "convivia," are springing up all over the region. Some ranchers are turning to organic, and/or grass-fed, not just to manage their lands and their herds better, but because they've discovered it makes long-term economic sense. Others are exchanging cattle for buffalo (American bison) because they withstand tough winters better than cows while being gentler on the land; on top of that their meat is very low in fat. Artisinal goat cheese producers are crafting cheeses that are being shipped all over the country and are winning awards in Europe. And organic nurseries are taking root in places previously unimaginable—and despite the challenges, they're thriving because their business is all about growing the right plant for their immediate region.

The sustainable food movement—developing across the Mountain West and promoted so sincerely by many of the best chefs in the northern Rockies—is so much about building and maintaining communities. And lucky it was for the

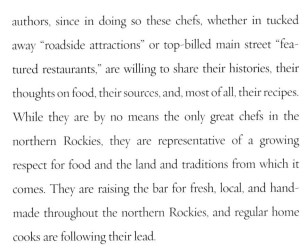

authors, since in doing so these chefs, whether in tucked away "roadside attractions" or top-billed main street "featured restaurants," are willing to share their histories, their thoughts on food, their sources, and, most of all, their recipes. While they are by no means the only great chefs in the northern Rockies, they are representative of a growing respect for food and the land and traditions from which it comes. They are raising the bar for fresh, local, and handmade throughout the northern Rockies, and regular home cooks are following their lead.

These chefs are helping build a movement, unwittingly or not, to offer a quality of life that has almost been relegated to a bygone era, the era Amy Jo grew up in back on that farm in Iowa, where relatives, friends, and neighbors were farmers— and all met up at the Stockyard Café. »⟶

ROADSIDE
ATTRACTIONS

LOG CABIN
CAFE
HOME COOKING

106

LOG CABIN CAFÉ

SILVER GATE, MONTANA

LocatED JUST ONE MILE from the northernmost—and by far most remote—entrance to Yellowstone National Park, Silver Gate lies on the border of Wyoming and Montana at an altitude of 7,400 feet in a valley surrounded by snow-covered 10,000-foot peaks. Tucked between Yellowstone's Lamar Valley, Montana's Beartooth Mountains, and Wyoming's Sunlight Basin and Absaroka Mountain Range, the town boasts direct access to some of the most remote and stunning wilderness in the world.

A summertime paradise of high country scenery, crystal clear lakes and streams, and wildlife so prolific that moose wander through town, Silver Gate and its sister town Cooke City become almost completely cut off in the winter. There's only one way in and that's through the park—more than fifty miles of daring, though spectacular, driving. If any one of the one

hundred souls who tough it out through the winter urgently need something from the outside world, they are far more likely to hop on a snowmobile and plow east for ten miles along snow-covered roads dodging buffalo and elk until they reach a parked car. From there, assuming the car starts in the sometimes thirty-below cold, they navigate over the incredibly scenic (though amid 12,000-foot peaks, it's icily dangerous, with hairpin turns and dramatic cliffs) Beartooth All American Road to reach the relative civilization of Red Lodge, Montana.

In 1977, Kay and Cecile King were teachers from Nebraska enjoying their summer freedom when they came across a For Sale sign on a Silver Gate restaurant housed in a 1937 log cabin. "A little old lady had owned it for thirty-four years," recalls Kay. "It was the hardest interview we've ever been through."

But the Kings were charmed by the vintage log building, its original furnishings, including handbuilt chairs and tables upholstered in the original red, yellow, green, and blue leather, Fiestaware pitchers, a Hoosier filled with antique glass bottles and cooking tools, and an ancient green machine for making malteds, still in use every day. The walls were covered with collectible fishing gear, bear skins, and moose, antelope, and mountain goat mounts. After promising that they would not quit their winter jobs (the old lady knew they wouldn't last if they planned to live there year-round), they closed the deal.

The food has always been American. A menu from the 1940s offers a chicken salad sandwich for eighty-five cents, a hamburger for a dollar, and a rainbow trout dinner with soup, salad, rolls, potato, dessert, and coffee for $3.95.

Today, breakfast features traditional fare: eggs and bacon, ham, homemade hash browns, fried trout, biscuits and gravy, pumpkin bread, and Log Cabin's famous pancakes made from a closely guarded sixty-year-old recipe that Cecile swore to keep secret when the former owner was—literally—on her deathbed. (That's okay, she says, because the recipe simply doesn't work at any other altitude.)

Lunch features sandwiches, homemade soups, and fresh-baked pies and cakes, while dinner steps it up with Alaskan king crab, Black Angus rib-eye, Cecile's signature chicken dish, and a sixty-year-old rainbow trout recipe. Every Saturday Kay rises extra early to prepare the weekly barbecue; he smokes babyback ribs and half chickens. Though he offers stuffed rainbow trout, Silver Gate, he says, is "steak country."

After thirty years of Silver Gate summers, the Kings are ready to retire and pass the legacy to the next generation. But they know things won't change too much. Says Kay, "This building is as old as I am and it will be here ten times longer." ⫸→

PAN-FRIED TROUT
AND HASH BROWNS

. . . .

The chefs at Log Cabin Café have been following this preparation for thirty years. The key is to get the freshest trout possible; Log Cabin Café's trout comes from spring-fed ponds in Idaho. The café's trout have skin on one side, but whole trout can be used following the same basic approach.

PAN-FRIED TROUT

1/2 cup flour

1/4 teaspoon salt

1/4 teaspoon pepper

2 egg whites

2 tablespoons water

1/2 cup bread crumbs

3 tablespoons butter, divided

6 trout fillets (8 to 10 ounces each)

Place flour, salt, and pepper in a wide, shallow bowl or plate. Combine egg whites and water in a second wide bowl. Place bread crumbs in a third bowl or plate.

Dip each filet in the egg white mixture, and then in the flour, and then back into the egg white mixture. Gently press into bread crumbs to coat both sides. Note: You can prepare this step ahead and refrigerate the breaded fillets.

Heat a flat grill or skillet (preferably cast iron) and melt about 1/2 tablespoon butter. Lay fillet back (skin) side down for 6 to 7 minutes. Place another 1/2 tablespoon butter in skillet, then turn fish onto the melted butter to get a nice color on both sides. Repeat with remaining fillets and butter. Serves 6.

HASH BROWNS

1 green bell pepper, chopped

1 small onion, chopped

6 large potatoes, pre-baked or boiled

2 tablespoons butter

Place bell pepper and onion in a blender or food processor and mince. Add potatoes and process until chunky and mixed together, but not mushy.

Heat large skillet (preferably cast iron) with 2 tablespoons butter until skillet is hot and butter is melted. Add potato mixture and spread evenly. Cook for approximately 10 minutes, turning just once but breaking up hash browns slightly.

LOG CABIN CAFÉ
PUMPKIN BREAD

4 eggs, beaten

3 cups sugar

I cup vegetable oil

I (15-ounce) can pumpkin

3-1/2 cups flour

2 teaspoons baking soda

I teaspoon salt

1/2 teaspoon baking powder

I teaspoon nutmeg

I teaspoon allspice

I teaspoon cinnamon

1/2 teaspoon ground cloves

2/3 cup water

Preheat oven to 350 degrees F. Oil and flour 2 loaf pans.

Mix together eggs, sugar, oil, and pumpkin. In separate bowl, sift together dry ingredients: flour, baking soda, salt, baking powder, nutmeg, allspice, cinnamon, and ground cloves.

Slowly add dry ingredients to the pumpkin mixture, alternating with water in 1/3 cup increments, mixing well after each addition. Pour into prepared pans.

Bake for 50 to 60 minutes, until firm to touch; cool on racks for 15 minutes. Remove pumpkin bread from pans and let cool further.

The Log Cabin Café serves this pumpkin bread warm, sliced in one-inch pieces and sprinkled with powdered sugar, with honey on the side.

THE PARK
CAFÉ

ST. MARY, MONTANA

THE PARK CAFÉ is way up north, by any definition. Located just twenty miles from the Canadian border in St. Mary, Montana, the restaurant perches on the edge of Glacier National Park, on the 1.5-million-acre Blackfeet Indian Reservation. For twenty-seven years, from May through Labor Day (opening and closing dates are sometimes determined by snowstorms), Kathryn Hiestand-Miller and Neal Miller have been dishing out homemade gourmet comfort food from the unlikeliest of kitchens.

Only tribal members can own property on the reservation, so Hiestand and Miller and their partners Rob Hiestand and Terry Offutt-Hiestand have a long-term lease on their restaurant; there they have created a respite for summer tourists, park service employees, hikers, Harley riders, cyclists, and RVers from around the world. The one thing these travelers

have in common is their luck in stumbling across The Park Café, an oasis of homemade meals in the land of factory-processed highway tourist food. (One guest en route from New York to Seattle by car told Hiestand-Miller that they had been traveling in "a culinary void" until they discovered the café.)

At the Park Café, the soups begin with vegetable stock, made in-house. Refried beans are made from scratch, from dried beans soaked overnight then slow-simmered with onions and spices. Every piecrust is hand-rolled on the counters of the cafe. Maintaining high-quality, fresh food in a remote tourist town is possible only through logistical gymnastics, careful ordering, and flexibility paired with resolve. If the crate of avocados comes in underripe, there will be no guacamole.

Hiestand and Miller have made a commendable commitment to reducing waste and recycling—no easy task in northwest Montana. They're also committed to creating "a fun, flexible, and fair" work environment. The staff, drawn by the lure of the spectacularly scenic 1,584-square-mile Glacier National Park, is a revolving host of outdoor bums (they're like ski bums, except they are climbers, whitewater rafters, anglers, and wilderness lovers). They work, live, cook, and hike together; in short, they eat well and they have fun.

The café serves breakfast—huevos rancheros, homemade granola, muffins, omelettes, veggie hash browns, and Fruity French Toast (served with strawberries, blueberries, and whipped cream, it's a favorite of biking groups). The pancakes, according to one professional chef, are "to die for. They're the best I've ever had—outside of my own kitchen."

For lunch and dinner there are soups, including mulligatawny, borscht, and chili. There's homemade salsa (so much, in fact, that one employee does little more than make salsa), burritos (such as "the Gypsy," with sweet potatoes), grilled chicken, hamburgers, and garden burgers.

The café's renown, however, comes from its pies: strawberry, raspberry, rhubarb, blackberry, cherry, apple, and various combinations thereof; lemon meringue, chocolate cream, and banana cream, all made fresh daily. After the "closed" sign is hung out at night, any leftover pie is devoured by appreciative employees.

Explains Hiestand, "As a child I liked it when my sister made pies for special occasions. I started by looking on the cornstarch box to see how much cornstarch to use. From there, I made lots of berry pies and then moved on to the cream pies. I love lemon meringue."

Hiestand says making pies is not really a choice for her. "I've gotta! Besides," she adds, "I do like making pies. My favorite pie is razzleberry, by far; next is strawberry-rhubarb. I know how many to bake because I have been baking them for twenty-seven years and customers are amazingly predictable! People eat less pie when the weather is really hot. And if there's an afternoon thunderstorm, people will stop in for pie. We sell more pies on holiday weekends— whole pies for those picnics! Old people eat the pies

that they shouldn't: cream pies. Young, hip kids like ice cream pie."

Hiestand buys her rhubarb direct from Hutterite farmers, the rest from more mainstream suppliers. And she does buy a lot.

"I buy 4,000 pounds of berries per summer—that is two tons. Yowza!" ⫸→

PARK CAFÉ PIE CRUST

. . . .

SINGLE CRUST FOR 9" PIE

1/2 cup flour

1/4 teaspoon salt

1/4 teaspoon cider vinegar

1 egg yolk, beaten

2 tablespoons canola oil

About 1 tablespoon water

Gently combine first 5 ingredients until dough begins to form. Add just enough water to hold dough together. Roll out on pastry cloth or very lightly floured surface until dough is about 2" larger than pan dimensions. Ease the dough into the pan and firm into place. Trim excess with a knife or kitchen scissors.

SUMMER FRESH STRAWBERRY RHUBARB PIE

. . . .

8 ounces (about 1-1/2 cups) strawberries, fresh or frozen

1 pound (about 3-1/2 cups) rhubarb, fresh or frozen

2/3 cup sugar

1 to 2 tablespoons cornstarch (depending on how dry the fruit is)

2 prepared pie crusts, uncooked

Preheat oven to 350 degrees F.

Mix fruit with sugar and cornstarch. Place in prepared pie crust. Lay second pie crust over fruit. Seal edges with fingers. Cut a few slices in the top crust to allow steam to escape during baking.

Bake at 350 degrees F for 50 to 60 minutes, until juice begins bubbling out the slits in the top crust.

Facing: Park Café's Classic Apple Pie

PARK CAFÉ'S
BANANA CREAM PIE

. . . .

3/4 cup sugar

3 tablespoons cornstarch

2 cups plus 2 tablespoons half-and-half or milk

Dash of salt

2 eggs, well beaten

2 tablespoons butter

1 teaspoon vanilla extract

3 to 4 bananas (about a pound), sliced

Prepared pie shell, baked for 15 to 18 minutes at
    350 degrees F and cooled

Make a paste with the sugar, cornstarch, and 2 tablespoons half-and-half. Pour the remaining 2 cups half-and-half into the top of a double boiler. Add the paste. Stir constantly until water in the base of the double boiler is boiling. Add hot water as needed to the base of the double boiler.

When the "pudding" is thickened and glossy, stir for a few more minutes and add the salt and beaten eggs. Cook, stirring constantly, until lumps are gone and pudding is thickened but not tough.

Remove from heat and add butter and vanilla. Stir well.

Fill prepared pie shell with sliced bananas. Cover bananas with pudding. Top with waxed paper. Refrigerate until cool, up to 3 hours.

PARK CAFÉ'S
CLASSIC APPLE PIE

. . . .

2-1/4 pounds Golden Delicious apples,
    peeled and sliced

1/2 cup sugar (can substitute brown sugar)

1 tablespoon cornstarch

1 teaspoon cinnamon

Prepared pie crust, uncooked

1/4 cup butter, chilled

1/3 cup brown sugar

1/2 cup flour

Preheat oven to 350 degrees F.

Gently toss apple slices with sugar, cornstarch, and cinnamon. Place apples into the prepared crust.

Mix butter, brown sugar, and flour and crumble with a pastry cutter or hands to get mixture into small bits. Spread over the apples carefully. Lightly press topping into apples.

Bake according to the following instructions:
"The important thing [for this pie] is in the baking. I hate undercooked apples and too many apple pies have undercooked apples. I bake the pie for 2 hours at 350ish with a large stainless steel bowl over the top not touching the pie. For the last 10 minutes I take off the bowl, turn up the heat a bit, and let the crumble topping brown."

—The Pie Lady, Kathryn Hiestand

Park Café's Classic Apple Pie

PINE CREEK
LODGE

CONGRATULATIONS
MISSY & SEBASTIAN
♫ MON HATCH ♪

PINE CREEK CAFÉ

LIVINGSTON, MONTANA

PINE CREEK CAFÉ is a sleepy kind of place. A bit off the beaten path (just off the main route from I-80 to Yellowstone National Park), it's nestled in the pines with a small creek splashing past. Located in Montana's breathtaking Paradise Valley, near Yellowstone National Park and historical Livingston, Pine Creek is what the word "getaway" should mean—a quaint, cozy, "Montana rustic" hideaway from which to enjoy the Rocky Mountains' spectacular beauty and all of its outdoor activities: fishing, hunting, hiking, horseback riding, whitewater rafting, and more. As they say at Pine Creek, "We're remote, but not isolated."

Pine Creek consists of a restaurant, five hand-hewn cabins, a gift shop, and grocery store. Nearby Livingston, Montana, is deceptively understated. It boasts the finest collection of art galleries for a town

its size anywhere in the West. The restaurant is a two-room affair that features interesting handmade food. There's outdoor music and a barbecue every weekend all summer long; throughout the winter, there's live music indoors and book readings by the fire. It's a true locals hangout, where neighbors, fishermen, ranchers, artists, and writers come in to get away from the crowds.

One of Pine Creek's signature dishes—and its most requested—is its Mexican-influenced Rainbow Trout Tacos. The chef fills three tacos with pan-fried, cornmeal-crusted rainbow trout fillets, Pepper Jack cheese, shredded lettuce, guacamole, and corn relish. This dish, served with refried beans and saffron rice on the side, was featured in *One Fish, Two Fish, Crawfish, Bluefish: The Smithsonian Sustainable Seafood Cookbook.*

Desserts, baked fresh daily, are of local legend. Cheesecake is an oft-requested item and variations rotate seasonally. Huckleberry is served year-round using frozen berries; other favorites include Lemon, and White Chocolate with Raspberries. In the fall, pumpkin evokes visions of swirling leaves and crisp, blue-skied days.

Some years ago, the owners restored a 1950s-style neon sign from a hotel in Bozeman. The soft glow from the lights lets neighbors know when the café is open. ⟫→

RAINBOW TROUT TACOS
WITH CORN RELISH

. . . .

Pine Creek serves their fish tacos with an avocado sauce made with sour cream and lemon juice—much like Sweetwater Restaurant's Avocado Aioli on page 212.

TACOS

12 taco shells

1 cup cornmeal

1/2 cup flour

2 teaspoons salt

2 teaspoons ground cumin

2 teaspoons chile powder

2 teaspoons garlic powder

2 teaspoons freshly ground pepper

2 teaspoons paprika

2 teaspoons dried thyme leaves

1 teaspoon cayenne

Canola oil

8 trout fillets (3 to 4 ounces each), skinned

3 cups shredded Pepper Jack cheese

Corn Relish

Avocado sauce or guacamole

3 cups finely shredded lettuce

1 lime, cut into wedges

Hot cooked beans and rice (optional)

Preheat oven to 300 degrees F to crisp taco shells.

Combine cornmeal, flour, salt, spices, and herbs. Heat small pool of oil in skillet over medium heat. Roll fillets in flour mixture and fry in skillet for 3 to 4 minutes per side. Cut off narrow end to create a rectangular and triangular piece. Working quickly, line each taco shell with 1/4 cup cheese and 1 rectangular piece and 2 triangular pieces of trout. Top each taco with Corn Relish, avocado sauce or guacamole, and 1/4 cup shredded lettuce.

Garnish with lime wedges and serve with beans and rice, if desired. Serves 6.

CORN RELISH

6 cups fresh or frozen corn

1 red bell pepper

1 green bell pepper

1 teaspoon salt

1-1/2 teaspoons celery salt

1/4 teaspoon cayenne

2 tablespoons dried mustard

3/4 cup brown sugar

1-1/4 cups cider vinegar

1 white onion, finely diced

Combine all ingredients except onion and bring to a boil. Reduce heat until liquid begins to evaporate. Add onion and simmer 10 minutes. Leftovers store well in the refrigerator.

PUMPKIN CHEESECAKE

. . . .

CRUST

2 cups coarsely chopped gingersnap cookies
  (about 30)
1 cup walnuts, chopped
1/4 cup butter, melted

Combine gingersnap crumbs and walnuts in a food processor. While machine is running, add butter in stream until combined. Press mixture into bottom and sides of a 10-inch springform pan. Set aside.

FILLING

1-1/2 cups pumpkin, cooked or canned
1 teaspoon allspice
2 teaspoons cinnamon
1/4 teaspoon nutmeg
Pinch of cloves
4 (8-ounce) packages cream cheese, softened
1-1/2 cups sugar
4 eggs
2 egg yolks
2 tablespoons flour
2 tablespoons heavy cream
Caramel sauce (optional)
Walnuts, chopped and toasted (optional)
Crystallized ginger, finely chopped (optional)

Preheat oven to 300 degrees F.

Mix together pumpkin and spices. Set aside.

Beat cream cheese until smooth. Add sugar slowly, beating to incorporate. Add eggs and yolks, one at a time. Add flour, and then pumpkin mixture and cream.

Place filling into crust and bake for 1 hour and 20 minutes. The center should still shake slightly. Turn off heat and allow cake to remain in oven, with door open, for an additional 15 minutes.

Refrigerate several hours or overnight before slicing.

Optional: When cake is cool, spread with a thin layer of caramel sauce and sprinkle with walnuts and ginger.

PLEASE
WAIT TO BE
SEATED
—Thank You!

WILLOW CREEK CAFÉ

WILLOW CREEK, MONTANA

WILLOW CREEK, MONTANA, is one of many towns in the northern Rockies that is surrounded by farms, bisected by little-used railroad tracks, landmarked by a towering grain elevator—and bypassed by a main road. The Willow Creek Café, located in a historic building, circa 1916, first started as the Corner Saloon serving country food to miners and ranchers. Since then, it has served time as a dance hall, barbershop, pool hall, and meat shop. Today, despite the local population numbering only 209, and despite the fact that one would have to be looking—hard—to find it, Willow Creek bustles six days a week.

On a random summer day at lunchtime, a local furniture maker stops in with her husband and some visiting friends, just for dessert and coffee. The two rooms—with their antique pressed tin ceilings

complete with bullet holes, floral wallpaper, wall mounts, and wood stoves—are busy. In one corner a long table is filled with ladies from the Red Hat Society, a national organization of women who don red hats and purple dresses and go out in public together to enjoy life; they are indeed enjoying life, as evidenced by animated gestures and much laughter. A few kids dressed to compete in a nearby rodeo bounce among tables visiting with neighbors while waiting for their parents to finish their meals. And servers maneuver among them bearing platters of ribs (some say they're the best ribs west of the Mississippi) and mouthwatering homemade desserts with such names as Russian Cream with Blackberry Sauce, Chocolate Heath Bar Crunch, and Red Raspberry Dana.

Owners Dean Mitchell and Tim Andrecik, partners for more than a decade, had both been chefs in the resort town of Big Sky, Montana, when they bought the café. According to Dean's wife, pastry chef Megan Higgins, their clientele followed them.

"We get a lot of local people," she says. "But Willow Creek is too small to really survive on the people who are here. We get a lot of people coming from Ennis, Butte, Dillon, and Bozeman. My husband and his partner are owners and also the cooks, so the food is very consistent. And," she adds, "they make the best ribs in the world. That's what brings them in."

People may come for the ribs, but they stay for Higgins' desserts, all made by hand and varying daily. "I make about twenty cakes, depending on the season. In the winter I serve more things like Hazelnut Cake with Mocha Mousse and Chocolate Bread Pudding with Orange Crème Anglaise. In the summer I make a frozen Lime Hazelnut Torte that I rarely make in the winter. After all these years I know what sells. The favorites are the Chocolate Heath Bar Crunch and Cheesecake with Berry Sauce."

As for her Orange-Poppyseed Cake with Buttercream Frosting, Higgins says, it's so special it has its own call list. "People want to know when I'm making it." »→

GRILLED CURRIED CHICKEN BREAST WITH CILANTRO-YOGURT SAUCE

6 boneless and skinless chicken breasts

1/2 cup olive oil

1/4 cup curry powder

6 onion sandwich buns

6 thick tomato slices

Cilantro-Yogurt Sauce

Spray or brush chicken breast with olive oil and cook on a grill. Just before chicken is done, spray or brush with oil again and sprinkle with curry powder. (Curry powder will burn if used at the beginning of the grilling.)

Serve chicken on grilled onion sandwich bun, topped with a tomato slice and a dollop of yogurt sauce. Serves 6.

CILANTRO-YOGURT SAUCE

1 cup plain yogurt

1/4 cup (or more) cilantro, chopped

1/2 cup red onion, finely diced

2 teaspoons lemon juice, freshly squeezed

1 dash hot sauce

Salt and pepper to taste

Mix together all ingredients.

SPINACH & POTATO SOUP

1/2 cup diced carrot

1/2 cup diced celery

1/2 cup diced onion

2 tablespoons butter

2 cloves garlic, minced

8 cups chicken stock

2 russet potatoes, peeled and diced

2 Yukon gold potatoes, diced

4 cups spinach, chopped

1 cup shredded Monterey Jack cheese

2 dashes Worcestershire sauce

2 dashes hot sauce

Salt and pepper to taste

Sauté carrots, celery, and onion in butter until tender. Add garlic and cook for 1 minute. Add stock and potatoes. Bring to a simmer. Add spinach. Cook until potatoes are tender but not falling apart. Add cheese, Worcestershire sauce, hot sauce, salt, and pepper. Stir continuously so cheese doesn't stick to the bottom of the pot.

Take out 1/3 of the soup and puree it in a blender; return pureed soup to the soup pot. Stir and serve. Serves 6 to 8.

ORANGE-POPPYSEED BUTTERCREAM CAKE

. . . .

1-3/4 cups cake flour

I cup plus 2 tablespoons granulated sugar

I teaspoon baking soda

1/4 teaspoon salt

1/2 cup butter

2 tablespoons orange juice

2 tablespoons orange liqueur

I teaspoon grated orange zest

3/4 cup sour cream, divided

3 eggs

3/4 teaspoon vanilla

3/4 teaspoon orange extract

1/4 cup poppyseeds

Buttercream Frosting

Preheat oven to 350 degrees F.

Grease bottom and sides of two 9-inch cake pans. Line the bottom with parchment paper and grease the paper.

Sift together the flour, sugar, baking soda, and salt. In a separate bowl, beat the butter; set aside. Combine orange juice, liqueur, zest, and 1/2 cup sour cream. In another bowl, combine eggs, 1/4 cup sour cream, vanilla, and orange extract. Add butter and orange juice mixtures to flour mixture. Beat on medium speed for 75 seconds. Add egg mixture in 3 batches, beating for 15 seconds with each addition. Fold in poppyseeds.

Divide batter evenly between 2 pans and bake in the middle of the oven for 25 to 30 minutes, or until a toothpick inserted in the cake comes out clean. Cool completely.

To assemble cake: Place one cake layer on cake plate and spread about 1 cup of buttercream frosting over entire surface. (Frosting must be at room temperature to spread easily and not tear the cake.) Place second cake layer on top of frosting and cover with about 1 cup frosting. Use remaining buttercream frosting to ice the sides of the cake.

BUTTERCREAM FROSTING

6 egg yolks

I cup sugar

1/4 cup corn syrup

2 tablespoons water

I pound butter, softened

2 teaspoons orange extract

I tablespoon grated orange zest

Beat egg yolks until light yellow and thick (5 to 7 minutes with paddle attachment on a mixer).

While eggs are beating, stir together in a small pot the sugar, corn syrup, and water. Mixture will be thick and somewhat "dry." Heat mixture over low heat, without stirring, until sugar is dissolved. Brush down sides of pot with water to prevent the syrup from crystallizing. Bring to a low boil and remove from the heat. *Take care with this hot syrup; it will make a nasty burn if it comes in contact with your skin!*

With the beater still going, add hot sugar syrup in a thin stream to the eggs. Beat until cooled, occasionally scraping down the sides of the bowl with a spatula.

When sugar and egg mixture cools to room temperature, beat in softened butter, 1 tablespoon at a time. When the butter is fully incorporated, beat in orange extract and zest.

Bunnery
RESTAURANT

Bakery, Coff
& Take-Ou

ESPRESSO

THE BUNNERY

JACKSON, WYOMING

J ACKSON HOLE is known the world over for its very westernness: the massive antler arches marking its town square; the famous Million Dollar Cowboy Bar, whose bar seats are real saddles; its Old West wooden sidewalks; and the jaw-droppingly scenic Teton Mountains. The unassuming Bunnery Restaurant, with its wood tables and booths, blue-checked curtains, and utilitarian white china, provides a restful contrast from the valley's larger-than-life expectations. Simply put, you could be Anywhere, USA.

This sense of familiarity, combined with wonderfully satisfying meals, ensures that the Bunnery draws crowds year round—but especially in the summer, and especially at breakfast time. Since 1975, when it was opened as Bru's Buns just two blocks from its current location, locals and visitors alike have flocked to the Bunnery for its breads and pastries, baked fresh daily, its housemade granola, its huge omelettes, flaky biscuits, and tender pancakes. Most summer days the

line goes right out the door and along the wooden boardwalk that skirts the outdoor seating area. Says longtime Bunnery manager Tony Labbe, on one July Fourth the Bunnery served a stunning 1,300 meals, half of which were breakfast.

Over the years the Bunnery has been mentioned in publications ranging from the *New York Times* to *Bon Appetit*. In 2007, *Mountain Living Magazine* bestowed its "Best Bakery in the Rocky Mountains" on the Bunnery.

Thanks to technology one no longer has to travel to Wyoming to bring home a bit of Jackson. The Bunnery maintains a Web site. Now customers are a click away from cinnamon bread, granola, huckleberry jam, Teton wildflower honey, the Bunnery's OSM bread mix, pancake and waffle mix, huckleberry-honey dill mustard—and, of course, buns.

The site also offers The Bunnery cookbook; fittingly titled *Get Your Buns in Here,* the book features recipes for hot cross buns, carrot cake, coconut bread, and sweet potato muffins.

For regular visitors who travel to Jackson for its world-class skiing, or for its fly fishing, whitewater rafting, dude ranching, or Yellowstone touring, a trip to the Bunnery can become an annual rite. As one www.tripadvisor.com reviewer put it, "When you consider the thousands of miles separating Central Texas from Jackson, Wyoming, you will understand why one might not want to make the trip too often. Then again, when your kids' favorite place for breakfast in the entire world is The Bunnery, you simply must return." ⟫→

HUEVOS
RANCHEROS

· · · · · · · · · · ·

2 medium potatoes, peeled and shredded

2 corn tortillas

1/2 cup grated cheddar cheese

1/2 cup black beans

4 eggs

1/4 cup salsa

1/4 cup sour cream

1/4 cup guacamole

Pinch of alfalfa sprouts for garnish

Fry the potatoes in a pan; set aside and keep warm.

Warm tortillas in a large skillet by setting in pan so tortillas overlap.

Divide cheese between the tortillas to melt. Layer the black beans over the cheese.

Fry eggs in a separate pan, and then lay them gently over the beans.

Place the above onto plate, then scoop on top the salsa, sour cream, and guacamole. Place the potatoes on side of plate and garnish with sprouts. Serves 2.

THE BUNNERY
COFFEE CAKE

. . . .

2-1/4 cups flour

3/4 cup sugar

3/4 cup brown sugar

1/2 teaspoon salt

1 teaspoon cinnamon

3/4 cup oil

1 cup pecans, chopped

1 cup buttermilk

1 egg, beaten

1 teaspoon baking soda

1 teaspoon baking powder

Preheat oven to 350 degrees F.

Mix flour, sugars, salt, cinnamon, and oil together in a large bowl. Remove 3/4 cup batter to a smaller bowl and add pecans. Mix well and set aside.

Add the remaining ingredients to the remaining mixture. Mix to combine (small lumps are okay). Pour batter into a well-greased 8 x 8-inch pan. Sprinkle the pecan mixture evenly over the surface.

Bake for 40 to 45 minutes, until a toothpick or knife inserted into center comes out clean.

YESTERDAY'S CALF-A

DELL, MONTANA

Yesterday's Calf-a really is in the middle of nowhere, off a north-south interstate little used except by truckers, sixty miles south of the I-90 as it runs between Bozeman and Butte. Dell, Montana, population 422, is just a glimpse off the highway, buffeted east and west by the Beaverhead National Forest and the remote Centennial Valley.

Nevertheless, it's a regular stop for truckers, travelers, and tourists heading north or south in the region. From the highway, travelers moving at seventy-five miles per hour have enough time to notice something unusual, hit the brakes, and still make the turn. At first glance, it's "Junk yard or museum? Wait, it's a schoolhouse. No, it's got a sign saying it's a . . . Must be a café!"

Yesterday's Calf-A is in a little 1890s red brick schoolhouse, surrounded by mementos of the past and filled with memorabilia collected or inherited

over the years: wagon wheels, a railroad crossing sign, the original school bell. And that's just the outside. Inside, the décor speaks of an era when the school was filled with beaten brown wood desks lined up in neat rows, schoolmarms wearing glasses and holding pointers in their hands. The sign is hand-painted, and not by a professional; the waitresses wear aprons and a warm smile. The specials and desserts are written on the schoolroom's original chalkboard, with a large

American flag hanging above.

Owner Linda Marxer, who grew up on a ranch near Browning, Montana, bought the café in 2002. Of the décor, she says, "Some of it is family stuff, some of it is what people have brought in. It's a little bit of everything."

Judy Colwell, an Adventure Cyclist life member from the San Francisco Bay Area, riding with the Continental Divide Ride Dogs, stayed in Dell on one of her cycling trips. "We went there specifically to dine (um, a euphemism for 'wolf down as much food as possible') at Yesterday's Calf-A," she says. "While we were there the most interesting characters walked in:

"A short, thick man, barely more than five feet tall, with an oversized black cowboy hat low over his eyebrows, and wide belt—like the Shorty Sheriff in a cartoon.

"A gaunt-faced truck driver with a package of cigarettes rolled in his gray t-shirt sleeve (something I thought was just a bad stereotype joke) and slicked black hair.

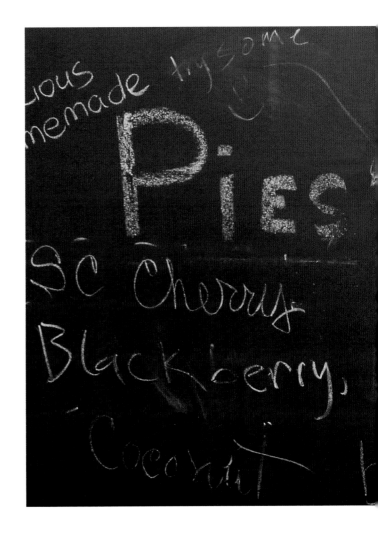

"Another driver, sporting a salt and pepper beard/moustache, wearing mirrored sunglasses (at eight p.m., inside the restaurant) mimicking the Georgia sheriff who, with sirens screaming and red lights flashing, pulls you over for going one mile per hour over the eighty-six miles per hour speed limit. He was well over six feet tall, lanky, wearing a suede vest with orange lining, and a light beige Stetson. Cowboy boots, of course."

Linda Marxer, asked about her regulars, says, "Our truckers are our family. Without them I wouldn't have a business."

At Yesterday's Calf-A, everything is "from scratch," even the french fries. Pies, a Calf-A specialty, are made from hand-worn recipes written on index cards and kept in a battered metal box. Whether truckers on their regular weekly route, or first-timers who glimpsed the café while speeding past, all naturally gravitate to the homemade doughnuts, made fresh every morning, sold out by lunchtime—and speaking of a bygone era. »→

YESTERDAY'S
CALF-A HOMEMADE
DOUGHNUTS

. . . .

At Yesterday's, this dough is also used to make a homey white bread.

1 tablespoon yeast
1-1/2 cups warm water
1 tablespoon oil
1 teaspoon salt
1/4 cup sugar
3 to 4 cups flour
Oil or fat for frying

Dissolve yeast in warm water. Stir in oil, salt, sugar, and 2 cups flour. Beat until smooth. Mix in enough remaining flour to make dough easy to handle.

Turn dough out onto a lightly floured surface. Knead until smooth and elastic, about 5 minutes. Place in greased bowl; turn greased side up. Cover; let rise in warm place until doubled in size, about 1-1/2 hours.

Punch down dough. Let rise again until almost double, about 30 minutes.

Roll dough 3/8 inch thick on lightly floured surface. Cut dough with floured doughnut cutter. Let rise on board until double and very light, 30 to 45 minutes. (Leave dough uncovered so crust will form on dough).

Heat 3 to 4 inches oil or fat to 375 degrees F in deep fat fryer or skillet. Drop doughnuts into hot oil. Turn doughnuts as they rise to surface. Fry 2 to 3 minutes or until golden brown on both sides.

Carefully remove from fat; do not prick the surface. Drain. While warm, roll doughnuts in sugar, or, if desired, frost or glaze. Makes about 2 dozen.

MAIN STREET
MENUS

PEARL CAFÉ & BAKERY

MISSOULA, MONTANA

MISSOULA is a quaint university town nestled in a valley along the west slope of the Continental Divide. The "Clark Fork," as Montanans refer to it, is the river made famous by Norman Maclean's *A River Runs through It.* And this river is central—literally and figuratively—in the life of Missoulans.

University of Montana students walk the river path to class; concerts and festivals are held on the river's bank; and some of the best dining in Montana takes place within sight of the water. Pearl Café & Bakery is located in downtown Missoula, on a quiet side street off the main drag, just north of the Clark Fork River.

Pearl's motto—"country fare with a city flair"—captures the essence of the café. Her menu is a bold combination of local meat and produce served in a style more common to a bistro in Paris than a diner in Montana. Guests are transported once they enter the door. Fancy by Montana standards, Pearl's is all white tablecloths, a roaring fire, and lots of glasses and silverware gleaming against a backdrop of brick walls. A cozy bar near the entrance is so inviting that many couples never make it to a table, opting for service on a stool instead for a convivial, neighborly experience. For a quieter, more private meal, the main dining room has booths along one wall and not more than ten tables; for an aerial view of upbeat young servers (looking a lot like University of Montana grad students), a loft overlooks the bar.

A fourth-generation Montanan, Pearl Cash says she went to France in the 1970s and "never really came back." She ate in as many four-star restaurants as she could and attended a small cooking school in Burgundy.

Upon her return, Pearl launched her first restaurant, in 1976, in the Bitterroot Valley; she's been behind the range ever since as executive chef and owner of some of western Montana's most critically acclaimed restaurants. She is the only Montana chef to have received the Best Northwest Award from *Seattle* magazine (July 1993). Pearl was profiled in

Bernard Clayton's *Cooking Across America.* That great chef named her "arguably one of the best young chefs in the country."

"I can't think of a place I'd rather be than in Missoula," she says. "It is so vibrant and dynamic. And we have the most interesting customers, from all over the world."

Setting the tone for fabulous service, Pearl often greets her guests at the door—that is, when she is not spending the evening in the heat of the kitchen. An extensive and intriguing wine list pairs nicely with a bold, interesting menu that combines European and Montanan influences in such dishes as Elk Osso Bucco; Bacon-Wrapped Rabbit with Rosemary and Wild Mushrooms; Savory Montana Pork Served with Braised Red Cabbage and Apples; and Smoked Bison Tenderloin with Zinfandel Huckleberry Sauce, Porcini Mushroom Aioli, Potato Gratin, and Crispy Leeks.

Pearl grew up on a small dairy farm in the Bitterroot Valley, south of Missoula. "It's only natural for me to be passionately interested in buying locally.

When I was growing up we raised almost all our food; we bought almost nothing." Today she buys as much as possible from local producers, which she admits is tough. After all, she says, "This is Montana"—prone to snowstorms in July and hailstorms in August.

She buys from Clark Fork Organics ("They provide us with incredibly beautiful fresh baby greens for the entire summer"), and Blue Willow Farms for delicate micro-greens, lemon verbena, basil tips, and the tiny flowers that Pearl uses as garnish. "Their attention to detail is second to none," she says. Pearl lauds the work of Western Montana Growers, a cooperative that provides an invaluable service to small Montana farmers and restaurants in the region. "They do what small farmers don't have the time to do: marketing and delivering." Pearl talks to WMG once a week to see what is available and then places her order, which is delivered to her door.

"They provide our inspiration for what we are going to serve. We get what we can get, anything at all, and make a recipe around it." »→

PEARL CAFÉ & BAKERY
VALENTINE'S DINNER
FOR TWO

· · · · · · · · · · ·

Serves 2

**SMOKED SALMON SALAD
WITH HEART BEETS, LEMON VINAIGRETTE,
AND HORSERADISH CREAM**

CURRIED ASPARAGUS SOUP

**BEEF TENDERLOIN STEAKS
WITH MUSTARD AND TARRAGON SAUCE**

**THYME-ROASTED NEW POTATOES
AND SAUTÉED SPINACH**

**WARM CHOCOLATE CHIP TARTS
WITH ORANGE SUPREMES
MARINATED IN ORANGE LIQUEUR**

SMOKED SALMON SALAD WITH HEART BEETS, LEMON VINAIGRETTE, AND HORSERADISH CREAM

· · · · · · · · · · · · ·

1 medium beet

1 teaspoon olive oil

3 tablespoons Lemon Vinaigrette

1/4 cup sour cream

1-1/2 teaspoons horseradish

1/4 teaspoon salt

2 cups mixed baby greens

3 ounces sliced smoked salmon

Zest of 1 lemon

Preheat oven to 350 degrees F. Rub beet with oil, wrap in foil, and roast for one hour. Check for doneness by inserting a knife into the beet; there should be only slight resistance. Let cool. Peel beet and cut into small cubes, or slice and cut with a heart-shaped cookie cutter to make "heart beets." Toss with 2 tablespoons Lemon Vinaigrette and set aside.

Make horseradish cream by combining sour cream with horseradish and salt.

Toss greens with the remaining Vinaigrette; place at the top half of 2 dinner-size plates. Spoon horseradish cream along one side of each plate. Arrange heart beets over the cream. Arrange the salmon in a loose rose shape in the center (partially on the cream, partially on the greens). Sprinkle the lemon zest over all and serve.

LEMON VINAIGRETTE

1-1/2 teaspoons Dijon mustard

1/4 teaspoon salt

3 turns of the pepper mill
   (or 1/8 teaspoon black pepper)

2 tablespoons lemon juice

1 clove garlic, pressed

1/2 cup extra virgin olive oil

Whisk together mustard, salt, pepper, lemon juice, and garlic. Whisk in olive oil. Stir or shake before using.

CURRIED ASPARAGUS SOUP

· · · · · · · · · · · ·

2 tablespoons butter

1/2 cup chopped onion

1 clove garlic

2 teaspoons curry powder

2 cups chicken broth

12 ounces fresh asparagus (approximately
  1 bunch), chopped

3 tablespoons half-and-half

2 ounces fresh crabmeat (optional)

Fresh chives for garnish

Melt butter in saucepan and sauté onion, garlic, and curry powder until softened. Add broth and bring to a boil. Add asparagus and cook until just tender, about 10 minutes. Blend in blender with half-and-half until just smooth. Strain through a mesh strainer to remove any fibers. Taste for seasoning and add, if necessary, up to 1/2 teaspoon salt, or more curry, broth, or half-and-half, depending on consistency. If using crab, add when reheating gently. Garnish with chives.

BEEF TENDERLOIN STEAKS WITH MUSTARD AND TARRAGON SAUCE

· · · · · · · · · · · ·

2 tenderloin steaks, salted and peppered

1 tablespoon butter

1 tablespoon oil

1/4 cup cognac

1/4 cup beef stock

1/4 cup dry white wine

1/2 cup heavy cream

2 tablespoons Dijon mustard

1/2 teaspoon minced garlic

1 tablespoon fresh tarragon

Salt and pepper to taste

Cherry tomatoes

Salt

Butter

Fresh tarragon sprigs for garnish

Sauté steaks to desired doneness in the butter and oil. Keep warm.

Deglaze the pan with the cognac and stock and reduce to a few tablespoons. Add the wine and reduce by half. Add the cream and reduce until it begins to thicken. Swirl in the mustard, garlic, and tarragon.

Heat briefly, taste for seasoning, pour over steaks, and serve with Thyme-Roasted New Potatoes, Sautéed Spinach, and cherry tomatoes, tossed for 2 minutes in a warm skillet with salt and butter. Garnish with fresh tarragon.

THYME-ROASTED NEW POTATOES

· · · · · · · · · · · ·

30 new potatoes

8 tablespoons (1 stick) unsalted butter

1/2 cup chopped fresh thyme

Salt and pepper, to taste

Preheat oven to 375 degrees F.

Clean potatoes and allow to dry. Melt butter in a heavy casserole or roasting dish. Add potatoes and stir to coat with butter. Add thyme leaves and season with salt and pepper to taste.

Roast in preheated oven for 30 to 45 minutes. Stir potatoes occasionally. Serve immediately.

SAUTÉED SPINACH

· · · · · · · · · · · ·

2 tablespoons olive oil

1-1/2 pounds baby spinach leaves

2 tablespoons lemon juice

Salt and pepper to taste

Wash the spinach well.

Heat olive oil in a large skillet over medium heat. Add spinach in batches. Quickly sauté just until wilted and a deep, vibrant green. Stir in lemon juice. Season with salt and pepper. Serve immediately.

WARM CHOCOLATE CHIP TARTS WITH MARINATED ORANGES

. . . .

1 large orange (a pink-fleshed blood orange,
    if possible), peeled, segments removed

4 tablespoons Grand Marnier or other
    orange liqueur, divided

3 ounces bittersweet chocolate, chopped

8 tablespoons best quality unsalted butter

4 large eggs

1/8 teaspoon salt

1 tablespoon corn syrup

1 cup sugar

3 tablespoons half-and-half

3/4 teaspoon vanilla

6 ounces best quality bittersweet chocolate chips

6 (4-inch) Tart Crusts (or one 9-inch crust),
    baked and cooled

Whipped cream or vanilla ice cream

Preheat oven to 325 degrees F.

In small bowl gently toss the orange segments with 2 tablespoons orange liqueur. Set aside to marinate.

Melt chocolate and butter together. Whisk the eggs, salt, corn syrup, sugar, half-and-half, vanilla, and remaining orange liqueur together in a bowl. Whisk this mixture into the melted, still-warm chocolate-butter mixture.

Sprinkle the chips evenly over the bottoms of the pre-baked tart crusts. Pour the chocolate mixture over the chips.

Bake for 20 to 25 minutes, until barely set. Allow to rest at room temperature. Reheat briefly, if needed; tarts should be served barely warm.

Serve with the marinated oranges and whipped cream or vanilla ice cream. Serves 6.

TART CRUST

1-1/2 cups flour

2 tablespoons sugar

Pinch salt

3/4 cup unsalted butter, cold, cut into 8 pieces

Preheat oven to 375 degrees F.

Mix together flour, sugar, and salt in a food processor. Add butter and mix until dough forms. Press into six 4-inch tart pans with removable bottoms, or one 9-inch tart pan with removable bottom.

Bake for 15 to 18 minutes until golden brown. Cool completely before filling.

LA CENSE
MONTANA
GRASS-FED
BEEF

DILLON, MONTANA

La Cense Montana breeds happy, healthy cows. Situated along the western slope of the Blacktail Mountains and covering 122 square miles, the ranch has been in continual operation since 1869, making it one of Montana's oldest and most historic cattle ranches. And that's fitting, because owners William Kriegel and Loraine Miller like to do things the old-fashioned way in the most progressive manner possible.

It's old fashioned in that there are no feedlots, no grain-fattening, no antibiotics, no synthetic hormones, and no stress-inducing final transfer to a "processing facility." At the same time, Miller explains, "La Cense Montana is one of the most progressive ranches in the West today. Yes, we embrace the old-fashioned values of pure and natural food, but it is our application of progressive breeding and ranching techniques that makes La Cense work. We are seen as the future of the beef industry, not the past."

Kriegel purchased the ranch in 1999. "My intention was to run the ranch but keep it as natural, efficient, and/or economically sustainable as possible," he recalls. "We thought we could produce meat the way it was done in the old time. We studied different methods around the world. We do rotation grazing, which is very simple: you divide big pastures into small pastures, maybe eighty acres, and put the cows in it for one day. If they only eat the top of the plant, it can grow back in eighteen to twenty days. If they eat the full plant, it takes forty-five to fifty days. The cow can come back to the same pasture five or six times a season; the other way only twice. It's a better use of the land and water: there's no cutting so there's less pollution, and you give the cow the best food you can."

Loraine Miller explains, "Grass is the natural diet

of cows—not grain! When a cow eats grain, even organic grain, you are creating an unnatural situation. The ranching techniques we use for our grass-fed cows include pasture rotation (how often, how many), the mix of grasses (how much alfalfa, how much bunchgrass, etc.), the age and weight of the cow when harvested, the length of the dry-aging period, and the hand-cutting craftsmanship. We even have changed the time of calving season to be in alignment with nature, which contributes to healthier cows. All this results in a healthier and better-tasting beef."

La Cense does not sell its meat wholesale, only direct to the customer through a Web site and from a shipping facility in Dillon. This involves educating the consumer as to why the beef tastes better. "Cows that are one hundred percent grass fed and grass finished exhibit a sense of 'terroir,' similar to wine from a specific vineyard," says Miller. "The unique climate of southwestern Montana, and the natural grasses and soil of the ranch, combine to provide a beef taste and quality that is distinctive."

It also involves educating the consumer as to the health benefits of eating grass-fed beef rather than grain-finished beef. These benefits are considerable. Southwest Montana is great cattle country, with a cool, dry climate and an abundance of native alfalfa and bluebunch wheatgrass. The resulting meat is lower in fat and calories than a typical cut of beef, and contains more beta-carotene, CLA (conjugated linoleic acids), and omega-3 fatty acids. Grass-fed beef is lower in fat even than organic beef, because organic beef is usually grain-finished and grain finishing builds fat. "This beef has less fat than chicken and more omega-3 than salmon," says Kriegel.

Not having to cut and feed hay, and not shipping cattle to another site to feed them grain for several weeks, saves on water, energy, time, and pollution, explains Kriegel. "We've been able to develop a strategy that protects the land, and is a better use of the land, and [in the end] you can sell something that is very high quality that the customer can enjoy." But the bottom line, Kriegel adds, is that it serves a growing trend toward more healthful food with known origins. "People want to buy from the source," says Kriegel. "They want to know how their meat's been raised and where it comes from." ⟫→

LONDON BROIL ROAST WITH BRUSSELS SPROUTS AND BLUE CHEESE

· · · · · · · · · · · ·

2 cloves garlic

I sprig rosemary

Salt and pepper

I (18-ounce) London broil

I pint Brussels sprouts

Extra virgin olive oil

I medium red onion, sliced in rings

1/4 pound Stilton or Roquefort cheese

1/2 lemon

Preheat oven to 400 degrees F.

Using a food processor or mortar and pestle, make a paste of garlic and chopped rosemary with some salt. Spread on the London broil and leave to marinate for at least an hour, preferably overnight.

Prepare the Brussels sprouts by removing any rough outside leaves, cutting them in half through the root base, and giving them a toss in olive oil with salt and pepper. Place them on a roasting pan and roast them in the hot oven for 25 minutes or until they are slightly caramelized and tender when probed with a knife.

Toss onions in oil with salt and pepper and roast in the same way as the sprouts. (This can also be done on the grill when you cook the roast.)

Preheat broiler or prepare barbecue (medium-high heat). Broil or grill steak until cooked to desired doneness, about 3 minutes per side for medium rare. It is important not to overcook the meat. In order to achieve the best results, let the steak rest well (no less than 10 minutes) before slicing it. This will help preserve the juices and allow the meat to relax. Thinly slice steak across the grain.

Toss the sprouts with the onion rings and crumble a bit of the blue cheese into the mixture. Season and add a bit of olive oil to help the ingredients marry. Squeeze in a bit of lemon juice as well. Set on top of the roast slices and serve. Serves 6.

CK'S
REAL FOOD

HAILEY, IDAHO

CHRIS KASTNER and his wife, Rebecca, co-owners of CK's Real Food, have worked together since 1978—a true sign of success in the high-pressure restaurant business. "I came here to ski," recalls Chris. "I started out as a dishwasher in Sun Valley; I really liked it in the kitchen. I had done as much college as I could without finding a direction. I thought this was what I was good at. It was hard at first; I worked three jobs—cooking, woodcutting, and snow removal. It was the hardest year I ever had."

But he stuck with it and made his name over the years as a gifted chef at a number of popular restaurants in the Sun Valley area, including longtime locals' favorite Evergreen. In the early 1980s, he spent a year and a half working as a chef in southern California, "a great learning experience," he recalls, but he couldn't wait to get back to Idaho—where he's remained ever since.

In 2002 Chris and Rebecca had been partners of a restaurant in Ketchum when they were bought out. They decided the time was right to strike out on their own; they purchased a corner property on the main street in downtown Hailey, which in the past decade has become the residential hub of the Wood River Valley as many local professionals have been squeezed out of pricier Sun Valley and Ketchum. A year later they opened CK's Real Food.

"Hailey was ready for us," Chris says. "They were ready to have a place to go. We wanted to be a small bistro-type neighborhood restaurant. We filled a niche here right away. And we get a lot of support from second-home owners when they're in town."

Their thirty-year working partnership still in effect, Rebecca runs the front of the house; she also develops the new dessert recipes and selects the restaurant's wines. Chris and Rebecca have two grown children who have long been involved with the restaurant: Gavin, who usually works the kitchen, and Simone, whose specialty is ice cream and sorbets. The Kastners are keen on local sourcing and using the freshest ingredients possible. Chris Kastner begins every description of his menu with a word about the ingredients. ⟫→

CHILLED EMMETT CHERRY SOUP

**TOMATO, GRILLED SWEET ONION,
AND WILD WATERCRESS SALAD WITH
ROGUE CREAMERY OREGONZOLA
VINAIGRETTE**

**ALASKAN HALIBUT WITH
GREEN GARLIC AIOLI, POACHED SHOSHONE
ASPARAGUS, AND IDAHO MORELS**

ESPRESSO GRANITA

CHILLED EMMETT CHERRY SOUP

· · · · · · · · · · · ·

Kastner loves the fresh tastes of summer, and its infinite possibilities. In summertime he takes his inspiration from whatever fruit is brought to his door.

"We always look forward to Idaho fruit season when Curtis from Waterwheel Farm brings cherries, peaches, apricots, and berries," he says. "This recipe has a fruit soup stock component and a fruit portion. It can be adapted for other fruits, such as peaches or nectarines, and these can all be enhanced by adding local berries. Just don't muddy it up with so many varieties that your taste buds get lost. Keep it simple: one star, and two or three bit-playing fruits at the most. If you have lots of fruit, freeze some extra. Excellent quality fruit, carefully frozen, will give good results, so you can treat yourself all year to a taste of early summer."

3 cups Fruit Stock

4 quarts fresh pitted cherries (ripe Bings are best),
    7 pounds before pitting

Kosher salt to taste

1 tablespoon balsamic vinegar

1 tablespoon lemon juice

Sugar (optional)

1 cup plain nonfat yogurt, whipped with whisk
    until smooth

Combine the stock and a two-finger pinch of salt with the cherries. Bring to a simmer for 25 minutes. Puree the soup and strain through a food mill or sieve.

Add the vinegar and lemon juice and a pinch more salt as needed; taste and adjust acidity with a little sugar if the soup is too tart or more vinegar if it is too sweet. It should be well balanced but more to the tart end of the flavor spectrum.

Serve in shot glasses with a few drops of yogurt drizzle on top for passed appetizers. For a more elegant look, serve it in a wide, low soup plate with a fun drizzle of yogurt on top.

FRUIT STOCK

1 tablespoon peeled and grated fresh ginger

1 star anise pod

1 (2-inch) cinnamon stick

1 serrano chile

1 lemon, zested and juiced

1 orange, zested and juiced

1 bottle Moscato or Riesling wine

6 cups water

1/2 cup sugar

1 vanilla bean, split down the middle

Combine ginger, star anise, cinnamon stick, chile, lemon zest and juice, orange zest and juice, wine, water, sugar, and vanilla bean in a nonreactive pot. Bring to a simmer and maintain it for 20 minutes. Strain the stock and reserve.

Make ahead and freeze in 1-cup containers or keep in the refrigerator for two weeks. Yields 9 cups of stock, enough for 3 batches of soup.

TOMATO, GRILLED SWEET ONION, AND WILD WATERCRESS SALAD WITH ROGUE CREAMERY OREGONZOLA VINAIGRETTE

· · · · · · · · · · ·

Chris Kastner on tomatoes: "Tomatoes come on in July in these parts. Glen Shepard from The Springs of Life farm in Hagerman, Idaho, is usually the first to show up with his. Judy Brossie from Ernie's Organics in Shoshone is there. Later in August, Dan Freeman of Shooting Star Garden from right down the road in Hailey comes around with an awesome selection of heirloom varieties. The most difficult to grow, but somehow he makes it happen. Go to your local farmers' market and get the best tomatoes you can. If you are lucky and have a pristine high desert spring-fed creek carpeted with lush emerald watercress, like we do, then by all means go pick some. Walla Walla, Maui, or Vidalia type sweet non-storing onions are best. And everyone is growing their own local sweet these days, so get what you can and then make this salad."

2 sweet onions, sliced 1 inch thick
Olive oil for brushing on onions, about
   1-1/2 tablespoons
1 tablespoon fresh thyme, chopped
Kosher salt and coarse black pepper
1 gallon fresh, washed, and spun-dry watercress
   or arugula

4 large bursting-with-juice local tomatoes,
core trimmed and sliced 1-inch thick
1 pound Rogue Creamery Oregonzola, or other great,
firm-textured, medium-intensity bleu cheese, sliced
1/2 inch thick
Oregonzola Vinaigrette

Brush onion slices with olive oil, and then sprinkle with thyme, and salt and pepper to taste.

Shortly before serving, grill the onions just enough to smoke and mark them, yet keep them on the crisp side of tender. Set aside at room temperature until assembly.

On a large plate, place a generous bed of cress or other spicy greens, two slices of tomato, a fat slice of cheese, and the onion slices, separated into rings across the top. Whisk the dressing and distribute it around the plate and over the salad. (Don't overdress; there will be enough dressing for at least 8 salads.) Sprinkle any remaining crumbled pieces of the cheese that are left over from slicing across the tops of the dressed salads.

OREGONZOLA VINAIGRETTE

1 clove garlic, smashed and minced
1/4 cup tomato meats scooped off the end cut
of the tomatoes (no skin), chopped fine
1/4 cup plus 1 tablespoon good quality red wine vinegar
1/2 teaspoon dry Coleman's mustard
1 pinch kosher salt
1 pinch pepper
2 pinches sugar
1 tablespoon lemon juice
1 cup good quality extra virgin olive oil
4 ounces crumbled bleu cheese

Place minced garlic and tomato pulp in the vinegar and let marinate for about 15 minutes.

Combine everything except the oil and cheese in a mixing bowl and whisk briskly for about 10 seconds, then whisk in the olive oil in a steady, unhurried way.

Note: This vinaigrette will not stay emulsified. It will separate, so it needs to be whisked well at dressing time. Then add crumbled cheese.

ALASKAN HALIBUT WITH
GREEN GARLIC AIOLI

. . . .

I lemon, sliced into quarters

I celery stalk, cut in thirds

1/2 carrot, halved lengthwise

I small onion, quartered

I bay leaf

I dry whole red chile

I tablespoon kosher salt

I cup Chardonnay

2 quarts water

8 halibut fillets (6 ounces each), skin removed

Green Garlic Aioli

The fish can be grilled or seared, but poaching imparts a moistness and delicate flavor that makes it worth the effort. If poaching, take out a wide sauté pan big enough to hold all the fish in one layer. Put the lemon, celery stalk, carrot, onion, bay leaf, chile, salt, and wine in the poaching pan; add 2 quarts water. Bring the pan to a boil, reduce to a simmer—barely a simmer—and maintain until serving time. Just a few minutes before serving, turn the pan up to boil, submerge the fish, turn it down to a simmer, and poach for 7 minutes, until just cooked through.

Place 3 asparagus on each plate. Divide the morels equally atop the ends of the asparagus; distribute the mushroom sauce on the plates, and then lay one piece of fish on each plate. Place a generous spoonful of Green Garlic Aioli on each piece of fish. Serves 8.

GREEN GARLIC AIOLI

Green garlic is garlic yanked out of the ground before it is fully mature. It has a sweet, garlicky taste without all the harsh and hot qualities of older, more jaded garlic.

1/2 cup green garlic, sliced, or 2 tablespoons
    ripe garlic, coarsely chopped

1/4 cup lemon juice

2 tablespoons white wine vinegar

I tablespoon water

I teaspoon kosher salt

Pinch cayenne pepper

I egg

2 cups canola oil or mayonnaise

Note: If uncomfortable with homemade mayonnaise due to raw egg concerns, leave out the egg and substitute purchased mayonnaise for the canola oil in the same amount, i.e. 2 cups. At the end of the food processing instructions, add the mayonnaise instead of the oil.

Combine everything except the oil or mayonnaise in the food processor. Pulse a few times to chop up the garlic well. Keep the machine running and pour in the oil or mayonnaise over a count of about 15 seconds. It should emulsify nicely. If it is too thick, add a little water to thin so it will not just sit on top of the fish. It should be sauce-like so that it will drape or drizzle. Adjust the seasoning with salt and lemon juice.

POACHED SHOSHONE
ASPARAGUS

. . . .

24 large, thick asparagus spears, tough ends trimmed
1 tablespoon kosher salt

Select a saucepot with a strainer or a steamer that will hold all the asparagus at once. Add water and salt and bring to a boil. Drop in the asparagus and cook for two minutes just barely to tender but hot through; drain.

IDAHO MORELS

. . . .

1 pound fresh morels, triple washed and well-drained
Salt and pepper to taste
4 to 8 tablespoons butter, divided
1/4 cup parsley, chopped

Put the morels in a large, dry sauté pan and turn the heat to high to cook all the water out of the morels. Season with a little salt and pepper. Add butter, 2 tablespoons at a time, and stir it in to make mushroom nectar. Add a couple ounces of the fish poaching water if it seems too dry. (You want thin, buttery nectar, not an insipid watery puddle. If you skimp on the butter, the body just won't develop in the sauce.) Add the parsley, and then taste and adjust with salt and pepper.

ESPRESSO GRANITA

. . . .

"Granita is fun and easy," insists Kastner, "but it does require your attention for a few minutes, every couple of hours throughout the day. You have to use a good strong espresso. Strong regular brew just won't do. If you do not have an espresso machine, have your local barista brew up sixteen ounces of your favorite blend. It can be decaf or regular. Be prepared to be refreshed and satisfied. This dessert is a great closer that doesn't leave you feeling like a fatted calf at the end of the day."

2 cups strong espresso, room temperature

1 cup sugar, divided

1/4 cup water

Combine everything in a mixing bowl or pitcher except for 2 tablespoons of the sugar. Mix well until sugar is dissolved, and then taste. It should be pretty sweet. Add the remaining sugar, if desired.

Pour the mixture into a flat, wide 2-quart sauté pan or other vessel that will allow the mix to be about an inch deep. Place it in the freezer. Depending on how cold your freezer gets, it will take 2 to 6 hours to freeze. Just check it every hour, and when it is almost frozen, take it out and chop it in the pan with a dough cutter or bench knife (sometimes this tool is called a board scraper). If it is really frozen solid, let it thaw for a few minutes until you can get the cutter through it. Chop it into about 1/4 inch pieces. There will be some bigger ones in there too, but that is

okay—you will get them the next time. Back in the freezer, let it set up again and in an hour or two repeat this chopping thing. Do this at least three times; four is better. You should end up with a scoopable, crystally, ice-like texture. When you like the texture of your granita, transfer it to a freezer container and scoop or spoon it into frozen wine glasses at service time. Top with some not overly sweet whipped cream.

ROLLING STONE CHÈVRE

PARMA, IDAHO

CHUCK EVANS grew up helping raise Charolais cattle on his parents' ranch in southwest Idaho, but as a fine artist he never considered staying there. He attended college and graduate school in Montana, then taught and practiced his ceramics in South Dakota and Minnesota. As he remembers it, "One day, I said, 'This is crazy—I don't like this administrative stuff.' The politics were inhuman; it was becoming impossible to teach." He and his wife, Karen, moved back to the family farm in Idaho. Once there, though, they discovered there was not much of a market for art pottery.

The Evans were already goat aficionados at that time, Chuck explains, but until then had only pursued it as a hobby. "We had been active in breeding, and very active in the American Dairy Goat Association.

At that time no one was concerned about the product. Milk went down the drain. I thought, 'This is a dairy operation.' We've always loved good food. Karen started making cheese and got very good at it. We started winning awards at the amateur level."

It wasn't long before the Evans decided to make a business out of goat cheese. He and Karen built a factory on their property with their own hands, and in 1988, they launched Rolling Stone Chèvre, in the process becoming Idaho's first goat-cheese producer.

"Rolling Stone is truly farmstead," Chuck explains. "We don't buy any of our milk. A lot of cheese people give up goats and buy their milk, but then they're at the mercy of their suppliers in terms of quality."

All Rolling Stone chèvre is made from milk from the Evans' own flock of several hundred Saanen goats. "As a breed, they're generally very calm and quiet. They do not exhibit the behavior people normally associate with goats. Cute is not their forte. They're very workmanlike. They will accept attention but don't require it."

Aided by a few part-time helpers, the Evans produce about twenty different items, including logs, fromage blanc, Italian-style hard cheese, specialized blues, tortas, and special-order items. Because Idaho has four definite seasons, subtle changes occur in the milk throughout the year. Due to these seasonal nuances, cheeses are paired to the season. All cheese is made using a traditional artisan approach, hand ladled, hand pressed, and then individually wrapped. Rolling Stone cheese is available to individuals and restaurants, but almost all of it is sold to retailers all over the country.

"Idaho is a wonderful place to raise goats, and Boise is a great distribution hub," says Chuck. "We've never used distributors, because our name is on the product and we want it to get to the customer in good condition."

Their approach—careful herd management, the use of only their own milk, and allowing the goats a natural pregnancy and lactation cycle—results in chèvre distinguished by its clean taste, mild flavor, and creamy texture. The recipient of many awards and accolades, Rolling Stone cheese was called "some of the finest goat cheese being produced outside France" by *Bon Appetit* magazine.

Chuck Evans doesn't have much time for his artwork these days, but he doesn't mind, he says. "To me, this is a fascinating mix of art and science. To some extent the goats are a very slow sculpture project." ≫→

These days you see goat cheese in tarts, tacos, and tapas. But the unique flavor of goat cheese warrants little fuss. Like most cheeses, goat cheese is best at room temperature, or even slightly heated, making it great to serve with roasted vegetables or on toasted baguettes.

BAKED GOAT CHEESE FOR ALL OCCASIONS

**8 ounces goat cheese, room temperature,
    cut into 4 equal portions**
**1/2 teaspoon fresh herbs, such as thyme, basil,
    and parsley**
Salt and pepper

Preheat oven to 400 degrees F. Place the cheese on a heavy baking sheet and sprinkle with herbs, salt, and pepper. Bake for about 3 minutes until cheese is warmed through but not spreading. Using a thin metal spatula, place slices on dressed bed of greens or on a cheese plate with crackers. Serves 4 or more.

GOAT CHEESE BALLS FOR ALL OCCASIONS

Goat cheese balls can be served with salads, on cheese plates, or tossed with olive oil and spread on bread slices.

8 ounces goat cheese, room temperature
**An assortment of flavorful accents, e.g., caraway seeds,
    ground cumin, paprika, fresh herbs, ground nuts,
    or chili powder**

Take about 1 teaspoon of goat cheese and roll into a ball. Roll in ingredient of choice, coating thoroughly. Refrigerate until ready to serve. Makes about 16 balls.

PAPOOSE CREEK

CAMERON, MONTANA

EAVE URBANITY. Fly to a small, quaint airport, and then get in the car and start driving: first on the interstate, and then on a two-lane highway. Watch the towns get smaller and smaller until they disappear altogether. Then drive for another hour, until you arrive at Papoose Creek.

Forty minutes west of Yellowstone National Park and adjacent to the Lee Metcalf Wilderness Area, Papoose Creek sits in the heart of the spectacularly scenic Madison Valley. Although located just off the road, it is masked by a grove of dense and shimmering white aspen. The lodge feels like home; set against a backdrop of soaring mountains, it has a big wrap-around porch overlooking a small lake—just the place to watch the sun set. The kitchen is open-style so guests can observe the chef at work; the long dining room table is perfect for family-style dinners. Several guest cabins, built from timber reclaimed from a forest fire and sprinkled here and there throughout the spruce forest, are spacious and refined. There are walking trails with signs interpreting habitat and plant life; there are riding trails that go deep into the mountains. The Madison River and Quake Lake are just a stone's throw away.

It's eco-luxury by design, according to owner Roger Lang, a former Silicon Valley high-tech entrepreneur turned environmentally oriented Montana rancher. "This is a lifestyle; it's a way of life. And I think we're making a real contribution as to how we coexist with wildlife and how to bring economic opportunity without carving up the land. Ecotourism and sustainability are huge, not just a trend. We think it's the answer to protecting the best in the West.

"We're still a working ranch, with 1,500 to 2,000 head of cattle. Some [beef] goes to the commercial market, some is grass-fed and grass finished in a cooperative effort with twenty ranches in the Madison Valley; that beef is served at Papoose Creek."

What might also appear on the menu at Papoose Creek are some eighty species of edible plants found on the ranch, explains Lang. "In the spring we put the leaves of glacier lilies in salad. They are so sweet and

go great with raspberry vinaigrette. We have a native buckwheat that can be ground up and made into pancakes. In the fall we collect mushrooms; we have forty-two species, though some are poisonous, and some are hallucinogenic—we don't feed those to our guests!"

The highlight of a stay at Papoose Creek is undoubtedly the weekly barbecue. A chuck wagon drawn by a team of Percherons carries guests to the cookout site, which varies according to the mood of

Lang and Executive Chef Michael Showers. From lush creek bottoms, Papoose Creek—combined with the historic Sun Ranch, also owned by Lang—extends across rolling grasslands, over rising foothills, and up to soaring 11,000-foot peaks. "There are so many wonderful places to take people, but we can't take them too far," he laughs. "After thirty minutes bumping on the wooden seats, it's not too fun anymore!"

The food, he says, is "chuck wagon fare: barbecued chicken, corn, beans, a fresh salad." Chef Showers sources the finest he can find in local ingredients: small-herd, grass-fed beef and naturally raised pork, lamb, and poultry. He's forged relationships with the area's organic farmers to fill the pantry with fresh produce; the lodge boasts an impressive eighty percent rate of local sourcing to create what they call "Sustainable Western Bistro Cuisine."

Lang says, "It's like what people out West would have eaten a hundred years ago." That is—if they'd had an inspired, enlightened chef dishing up their grub. ⟫→

PAPOOSE CREEK

SUMMERTIME

BARBECUE

. . . .

Serves 6

**CHARRED HEIRLOOM TOMATOES
WITH CHAMPAGNE VINAIGRETTE**

MAD VALLEY SLAW

PAPOOSE CREEK POTATO SALAD

**GRILLED SUN RANCH CHICKEN
WITH WHITE BARBECUE SAUCE**

HUCKLEBERRY AND APPLE CRISP

CHARRED HEIRLOOM TOMATOES WITH CHAMPAGNE VINAIGRETTE

1 large ripe beefsteak tomato, or substitute any large ripe red tomato (ideally, it should be at least baseball-sized)

1 cup extra virgin olive oil, plus extra for brushing on tomato

Salt and pepper

1/3 cup champagne vinegar

1 teaspoon Dijon mustard

1 shallot, minced

8 to 10 cups greens: arugula, frisée, or any peppery greens

Cut tomato into 4 to 5 slices; lightly season with olive oil, salt, and pepper. On a very hot grill, very quickly mark tomato slices (you just want a little smoke; don t cook the tomato).

Remove from grill and chill in refrigerator. In a stainless steel mixing bowl, mix champagne vinegar, Dijon mustard, and shallot. Slowly whip in olive oil (it s okay if it breaks; the chef actually prefers this vinaigrette broken). Add salt and pepper to taste.

Remove tomato from fridge, chop coarsely, and fold into vinaigrette.

Divide greens among 6 plates. Top with about a half cup of vinaigrette. Serve immediately.

MAD VALLEY SLAW

· · · · · · · · · · · · ·

1/4 head red cabbage

1/4 head green cabbage

1 red bell pepper

1/2 jalapeño pepper, finely minced

1 cup dried flathead cherries, slivered

Vinaigrette

Cut cabbages and red bell pepper into a very fine julienne. Mix all ingredients except Vinaigrette in a bowl. Pour Vinaigrette as needed over slaw ingredients and mix gently to combine. Salad should be coated, but not dripping.

VINAIGRETTE

1/2 cup buttermilk

1/3 cup plain yogurt

1/4 cup apple cider vinegar

1/4 cup apple juice

1/4 cup honey

1 tablespoon Worcestershire sauce

1 teaspoon caraway seeds

1 teaspoon ground cumin

1 teaspoon celery salt

A couple dashes of Tabasco

Salt and pepper to taste

Mix all ingredients together.

PAPOOSE CREEK POTATO SALAD

· · · · · · · · · · · · ·

2 pounds Yukon gold potatoes

3 eggs, hard-cooked and diced

2 ribs celery, diced

1/2 cup red onion, diced

4 green onions, thinly sliced

1 tablespoon stone-ground mustard

3/4 cup mayonnaise

1/4 cup sour cream

1 tablespoon apple cider vinegar

1 teaspoon Dijon mustard

2 tablespoons fresh dill

1 tablespoon flat-leaf parsley

1 teaspoon ground cumin

Salt and pepper to taste

Start potatoes in cold salted water, raise heat, and cook until fork tender. Drain and chill.

Once cooled, add eggs, celery, and onions and mix well. Add all wet ingredients and mix well. Gently fold in herbs and cumin. Season to taste with salt and freshly ground black pepper.

GRILLED SUN RANCH CHICKEN WITH WHITE BARBECUE SAUCE

· · · · · · · · · · · ·

2 organic roasting chickens (5 to 6 pounds each)

I quart buttermilk

5 to 7 bay leaves

10 peppercorns

2 parsley sprigs

2 fresh thyme sprigs

Salt and pepper

I recipe White Barbecue Sauce

Remove leg, thigh, and breast from carcass, separating the leg from the thigh (save carcass for stock). Place in shallow baking dish. Pour buttermilk over the top; mix in bay leaves, peppercorn, and herbs. Marinate for 24 hours in refrigerator.

Take chicken out of marinade and drain well (can pat dry). Season generously with salt and pepper. Place on medium-hot grill, skin side down, allowing time for chicken to mark (or else skin will stick). Turn chicken when marked and generously baste with reserved 1 cup White Barbecue Sauce. Keep flipping and basting until chicken is completely cooked. Serve immediately with the remaining White Barbecue Sauce, not used for basting, to pass around the table.

WHITE BARBECUE SAUCE

2 cups buttermilk

I tablespoon Dijon mustard

1/4 cup mayonnaise

1/4 cup sour cream

3 dashes Tabasco

1-1/2 teaspoons prepared horseradish

I tablespoon extra virgin olive oil

I tablespoon honey

I tablespoon lemon juice

1/4 teaspoon cumin

Dash cayenne

1/2 teaspoon chile powder

1/4 cup Italian parsley, minced

2 tablespoons fresh thyme, minced

I tablespoon garlic, minced

Salt and pepper to taste

In stainless steel mixing bowl, pour in all wet ingredients and mix well.

Incorporate dry ingredients, beginning with spices.

Refrigerate until ready to use. Reserve about 1 cup of sauce for basting.

HUCKLEBERRY AND APPLE CRISP

. . . .

TOPPING

6 tablespoons unbleached flour

1/4 cup sugar

1/4 cup brown sugar

1/2 teaspoon cinnamon

1/4 teaspoon ground nutmeg

Pinch salt

5 tablespoons unsalted butter

**3/4 cup almonds, crushed or pulsed in a food
    processor until coarsely chopped**

Place flour, sugars, spices, and salt into food processor and pulse briefly to combine. Add butter in stages and pulse until incorporated (should have texture of dry sand). Add the nuts and pulse again do not overmix. Refrigerate while preparing filling.

FILLING

4 baking apples (Granny Smith or McIntosh)

1 tablespoon unsalted butter

1 teaspoon lemon zest

Juice of 1 lemon

1-1/2 cups fresh Montana huckleberries

1/4 cup sugar

1/4 cup honey

2 tablespoons cornstarch

Preheat oven to 375 degrees F.

Peel, quarter, core, and cut apples into 1-inch pieces. Over low heat, place 1 tablespoon butter into a 4-quart saucepot; melt butter and add apples. Add zest, lemon juice, berries, sugar, and honey and cook gently over a low flame for 5 to 10 minutes. Add cornstarch and mix until combined. Pour fruit into 9-inch pie plate; distribute the chilled topping evenly over the fruit.

Bake for 40 minutes. Continue baking until the fruit is bubbling and the top is deep golden brown. Serve warm with vanilla ice cream or fresh whipped cream.

DEEP CREEK GREENS

LIVINGSTON, MONTANA

Dixie Hart, Manager of Deep Creek Greens in Montana's Paradise Valley, masterminds a modern miracle: she and her team grow not only herbs, produce, plants, and shrubs but also acres of tulips, dahlias, peonies, gladioli, lilies, and sunflowers, all sustainably grown in an area better known for its grizzly bears and wolves than its growers' bunches.

"We're in Paradise Valley, right off the Yellowstone River, on the west slope of the Absorkees but the east side of the valley," she explains. "We're Zone Four, but at five thousand feet, at the edge of the Rockies with wind, and late and early frosts and freezes . . . it's really kind of a challenge."

The climate is even more challenging for newcomers, she explains. "There's a lot of growth here; people come from all over the country and they aren't familiar with what grows here. We're very specific to our area.

Someone might come from the Northwest where rhododendrons are very popular. Rhododendrons won't do well here, but if they're looking for an early blooming shrub we might recommend lilacs. That's a big part of the service we provide—not selling things that we think our customers can't grow. We feature acclimated plants. We winter them over; some have been here for six seasons."

Deep Creek is an unlikely find on the edge of the Yellowstone wilderness. "It's so unexpected," Hart says. "People come here and their jaws drop. We have an eleven-acre garden field and a large perennial garden below. We have a state-of-the-art nursery and three greenhouses. The owners, Andreas Luder and Debbie Erdman, started this in the mid-'90s. It began as a hobby; now it's a hobby run amok. It's got a life and energy of its own."

Deep Creek Green celebrates the full cycle of plants, from garden to table. Thus, there's a commercial kitchen where four or five cooking classes are taught in the fall by visiting chefs. One class might be

devoted to breads, while another might involve preparing a five-course meal.

By fall, much of the garden has been put to rest. But for cooking students handling the garlic, the carrots, the turnips, the beets . . . they're learning firsthand the true meaning of "local sourcing." ⟫→

ROASTED BEET SALAD WITH ORANGES, BLUE CHEESE, WALNUTS, AND ORANGE-ANISEED DRESSING

. . . .

2 pounds red and golden beets, trimmed and scrubbed

3 oranges, peeled and sliced into 1/4" rounds

1/2 cup Orange-Aniseed Dressing

1/2 cup (about 2 ounces) blue cheese, crumbled

1/2 cup walnut halves, toasted

Preheat oven to 450 degrees F.

Place beets in a small roasting pan with about 1/8" water; cover loosely with foil. Roast for 30 to 45 minutes until tender when pierced with a knife.

When beets are cool enough to handle, peel them and slice into rounds. Toss gently with dressing to coat.

Arrange beet and orange slices on a plate. Drizzle with remaining dressing. Sprinkle the blue cheese and walnuts over the beets and oranges. Serve at once. Serves 6.

ORANGE-ANISEED DRESSING

Orange-aniseed dressing is great on steamed or roasted vegetables. It can be used as a marinade as well; combine vegetables and dressing and chill for up to a day.

6 tablespoons white wine vinegar

3 tablespoons frozen orange juice concentrate, thawed

2 tablespoons aniseed

1 tablespoon grated orange peel

1 tablespoon honey

1 cup olive oil

Salt and pepper to taste

In a blender, combine vinegar, orange juice, and aniseed for about a minute. Strain the mixture into a medium bowl, pressing on the aniseeds. Discard seeds. Whisk in orange peel, honey, and olive oil. Season with salt and pepper.

BROOKS
LAKE
LODGE

DUBOIS, WYOMING

THE HISTORY of Brooks Lake Lodge shares that of the other Great Western Lodges, like the Ahwahnee Hotel in Yosemite and the Old Faithful Inn in Yellowstone National Park. Built in a matter of months, from April to July 1922, for only summertime use, the massive structure, with its huge timbers, soaring stone fireplaces, and vaulted ceilings, exhibits the craftsmanship and artistry typified by the Arts and Crafts Movement. It shares with the movement a reverence for nature, and, like the other Great Lodges, an extraordinary setting. Rather than El Capitan or Old Faithful in the background, though, Brooks Lake Lodge, set at 9,200 feet in elevation within the wildlife-rich Greater Yellowstone wilderness, lies a quarter mile from crystal-clear Brooks Lake and has as its backdrop the dramatic Pinnacles—sheer granite cliffs rising to the sky. The Lodge is surrounded by the high peaks of the Pinnacle Mountains, the Continental Divide, Austin's Peak, and Brooks Mountain.

Originally built to serve as a way station for tourists traveling to see firsthand the geysers, hot springs, waterfalls, and buffalo herds of Yellowstone National Park, it later became a destination in itself as a guest ranch. It remained such throughout the heyday of the dude ranch era, when affluent eastern city-dwellers would travel west by train for month-long stays. Across the Rocky Mountains, the dude ranch business declined in the 1950s, but by the 1980s had experienced a resurgence with the popularity of such movies as *City Slickers*. Brooks Lake Lodge underwent a major renovation and in 1982 was listed on the National Register of Historic Places, noted for typifying "a distinct form of recreational retreat: a stopover along the road to Yellowstone National Park and a rustic resort hotel placed in a spectacular Rocky Mountain setting."

Brooks Lake today retains its yesteryear elegance along with its rugged outdoors orientation, but it displays all the panache of the contemporary upscale

resort that it is. Paradise for children and adventurers, with its riding, hiking, fishing, canoeing, pack trips and, with eight to twelve feet of powder each winter, snowshoeing, snowmobiling, dog sledding, and cross-country skiing—it also offers a luxurious spa, a lengthy wine list, and creative, mouthwatering fresh mountain cuisine.

Meals are served in the historic dining room, with soaring ceilings, warm lighting, polished wood floors, and a massive stone fireplace. Breakfast consists of fresh fruit, yogurt, homemade breads, malted waffles, and other original fare, while lunch can be gourmet boxed for all-day adventures. Dinner offers a daily changing menu of three-course meals using fresh ingredients and exhibiting a regional flair.

After a meal of Marinated Elk Rack with Huckleberry Sauce, or Poached Salmon with Cucumber, a nightcap outdoors on the porch—under a high-country night sky ablaze with stars—seems the only option.

As journalist David Brooks, writing in *Travel & Leisure* magazine, put it, a stay at Brooks Lake is "a high-end wilderness experience that marries the refinements of civilization with a reverence for nature. You think you're in the Siberian Gulag, and then they start treating you like you're Heloise at the Plaza." ⋙→

BROOKS LAKE
SUMMERTIME SPLENDOR
MENU

· · · · · · · · · · ·

Serves 6

GRILLED SQUAB SALAD WITH MANGO SALSA

**POACHED SALMON
WITH CUCUMBER VINAIGRETTE**

**MARINATED ELK RACK WITH
A WILD BERRY SAUCE**

HUCKLEBERRY SORBET

GRILLED SQUAB SALAD
WITH MANGO SALSA

. . . .

**3 whole squabs (may substitute small Cornish game
   hens, I to 1-1/4 pounds)**
I cup Greek Marinade
I pound mesclun mix or other tender greens
Mango Salsa

Marinate all three squabs in Greek Marinade for 1 to 2 hours.
Cut each squab in half. Place squab on a medium to hot
grill, turning as it browns, for about 10 minutes total, until
nicely browned and just cooked through (Cornish game
hens will take a little longer). Remove from heat and allow
to rest.

Place 2 to 3 ounces of mesclun mix on each plate. Place half
a squab on top of salad, and then spoon salsa over top.

GREEK MARINADE

I tablespoon lemon zest, minced
1/4 cup fresh oregano leaves, roughly chopped
I teaspoon salt
I teaspoon freshly ground pepper
Juice of I lemon
2/3 cup olive oil

Place lemon zest and oregano in a mixing bowl with salt and
pepper. Firmly mash the dry ingredients together. Add lemon
juice. Drizzle in the olive oil while whisking constantly. Use
mixture to marinate food for up to 3 hours before cooking,
or as a basting sauce when grilling or roasting.

Marinade can be stored in the refrigerator for several
weeks. Mix well before using.

MANGO SALSA

1/2 cup diced fresh pineapple
2 cups chopped mango
1/4 cup red onion, finely diced
2 tablespoons chopped chives
I tablespoon lime juice
1/4 cup honey

Mix pineapple, mango, onion, and chives in a medium bowl.
Mix lime juice and honey together in a small bowl. Pour over
fruit mixture and stir gently to coat.

POACHED SALMON WITH CUCUMBER VINAIGRETTE

· · · · · · · · · · · ·

2 cups white wine

12 cups water

3 bay leaves

1 teaspoon whole black peppercorns

2 tablespoons orange juice

6 salmon fillets (4 to 6 ounces each)

Cucumber Vinaigrette

Chopped seedless cucumber

Create a poaching liquid by combining the white wine, water, bay leaves, peppercorns, and orange juice in a large pot. Bring poaching liquid to a simmer, allowing time for the flavors to combine, about 15 minutes. Gently slide the salmon fillets into the poaching liquid. Let cook for about 5 to 6 minutes; there should still be a little pink in the middle. To garnish, spoon the vinaigrette on top of the poached salmon, and then add a few pieces of chopped seedless cucumber on top.

CUCUMBER VINAIGRETTE

1 cup chopped seedless cucumber

1 small shallot, diced

1 teaspoon dried lavender flowers

1 teaspoon dried or fresh dill

2 tablespoons red wine vinegar

4 tablespoons olive oil, or to taste

Combine first four ingredients in a medium bowl. Whisk vinegar and oil in a small bowl, and then pour over cucumber mixture. Toss gently to coat.

MARINATED ELK RACK WITH A WILD BERRY SAUCE

. . . .

6 pounds elk or beef rib rack, from standing rib roast

1/3 cup soy sauce

1/3 cup vegetable oil

1/3 cup red wine vinegar

1/3 cup pineapple juice

2 tablespoons ground ginger

1 cup dried bread crumbs or panko

1/2 teaspoon garlic powder

1/2 teaspoon onion powder

1 teaspoon salt

1 teaspoon black pepper

Wild Berry Sauce

Trim meat of any silver skin. Place in large, shallow pan. Whisk together soy sauce, vegetable oil, red wine vinegar, pineapple juice, and ginger. Pour over rib rack and let marinate for 6 to 8 hours. Combine bread crumbs, garlic powder, onion powder, salt, and pepper and scatter evenly onto a baking sheet.

Preheat oven to 450 degrees F. Take the rack directly from marinade and roll in bread crumb mixture until evenly coated. Place in large roasting pan.

Roast rack until internal temperature is 145 degrees F, about 30 to 45 minutes. After removing the rack from the oven, let sit for about 5 minutes.

WILD BERRY SAUCE

1 cup frozen berries (any combination of strawberries, blueberries, blackberries, or huckleberries)

2 cups red wine

1 teaspoon sugar, or more to taste

1 tablespoon cornstarch mixed with 1 tablespoon water (optional)

Place berries in medium saucepan. Add red wine until berries are just covered. Cook over medium heat until liquid is reduced by half. Let cool slightly, and then puree mixture. Strain into a second saucepan. Keep covered on low heat to prevent a skin from forming on the surface. Add sugar. Add cornstarch mixture and boil sauce to thicken, if desired.

HUCKLEBERRY

SORBET

. . . .

4 cups sugar

2 cups water

4 cups frozen huckleberries or blueberries

Make the "simple syrup": Combine sugar and water in a saucepan and bring to a boil. Remove from heat when all of the sugar is melted.

Puree the huckleberries in a food processor, thawed or frozen. When the simple syrup has cooled, combine with the pureed huckleberries and then place the mixture in an ice cream maker. Freeze according to manufacturer's instructions.

To serve: The sorbet can be spooned into a martini glass and topped with a fresh mint leaf. To add a little flair, pour some champagne into the glass with the sorbet.

SNAKE
CREEK
GRILL

HEBER CITY, UTAH

BARBARA HILL grew up far from the mountains, in Detroit. She was living in California, she recalls, when a girlfriend called her and said, "Come to Park City and be a ski bum." She did.

That was 1980. Since then she has worked for most of the top restaurants in Utah, including the restaurant at Deer Valley's ultra-luxurious Stein Eriksen Lodge, and Riverhorse, the spot of choice for power brokers at the Sundance Film Festival. For her last gig before going out on her own, she helped launch Robert Redford's Zoom, an always busy Main Street spot with great buzz from the moment it opened its doors.

Chef Hill and her husband, co-owner and restaurant manager Michael, chose an offbeat location for their first restaurant: Heber City, Utah. Only eighteen miles from Park City but a world away, the restaurant is located in Heber Old Town in a turn-of-the-century-styled building. Like Hill's food, the décor is welcoming and comforting: a copper-topped bar at the entry, antique wide-planked wood flooring, warm green and gold tones, wainscoting and cozy seating, and an assortment of the Hills' antiques and collectibles scattered throughout. Antique floral prints, black-and-white photographs, and a collection of antique silhouette thermometers decorate the walls, while white linen tablecloths and, in the summer months, sunflowers from the Hills' garden grace the tables.

Hill was always interested in cooking and earned an Associate's Degree from a cooking school in Michigan, but really, she says, "I learned my skills on the job." Barb is best known for her sophisticated comfort food: an ultra creamy and comforting Mac & Cheese; Crisp Corn Cakes in a pool of Sweet Pepper Cream; meltingly tender Baby Back Ribs with Mopping Sauce and Slaw; Barb's Mess O' Greens and Caramel Carrots; and Grilled Tri Tip with Wild Mushrooms and Crispy Hash Browns. Desserts are seasonal and mouthwatering: fresh fruit crisps, a peanut brittle and hot fudge sundae, and gingerbread cookie ice cream sandwiches with warm caramel dipping sauce.

"Heber was ready for that kind of food," Hill says. Her ever-busy tables have proved her right. The restaurant is popular with the serious Nordic skiers who stop in after a workout at Soldier Hollow, site of the 2002 Olympic Nordic ski competitions. "Those carbo-loaders keep fettucine on the menu year-round," she says. Other regulars include Park City locals and skiers, golfers from local courses, and, she says, "We have a strong customer base in Salt Lake."

The Hills source locally as much as possible. Morgan Valley Lamb provides organic lamb. "This lamb is off the dial!" Hill enthuses. A local heirloom tomato grower supplies the restaurant with tomatoes, including 1880s/early 1900s varieties such as the Flame Hillbilly, "a big beefy yellow tomato with mottled red streaking. It is not the perfect tomato, and that is what we like."

Hill's longtime pastry chef, Dean Hottle, a graduate of the CIA in Hyde Park, New York, worked in New York City for Brendan Walsh at Arizona 206 and The Elms Restaurant and Tavern in Richfield, Connecticut. He came to Utah to ski but ended up as Executive Chef at Stag Lodge in Deer Valley. Hottle has worked with Barb Hill at Snake Creek Grill since 1999 and is now in the process of taking over ownership. Barbara laughs, "I was the first person he saw, and the rest is history."

Under Hill, Hottle made all the desserts at Snake Creek Grill, such as the luscious Black-bottomed Banana Cream Pie, a summer fresh Strawberry Shortcake with Lemon Country Biscuits, and a wonderful Grand Marnier simple syrup that he puts on fresh strawberries. Hottle describes his food as "American comfort food with Southwest and Asian influences."

Hill will remain involved with the restaurant, supplying organic produce and sunflowers from her garden. She says Hottle and she have a similar style, which she calls "Bold Unpretentious." More importantly, she adds, "Dean cooks from the heart." ⫸→

SNAKE CREEK GRILL'S
ALL-SEASON
COMFORT FOOD

· · · · · · · · · · ·

Serves 6

SNAKE CREEK GRILL ONION SOUP

**BABY SPINACH SALAD WITH POMEGRANATE
SEEDS AND HONEY-BALSAMIC VINAIGRETTE**

**BLUE CORNMEAL CRUSTED RED TROUT
WITH TOMATILLO-CHIPOTLE SAUCE
AND CHIPOTLE CREMA,
SERVED WITH CHILI CORN CUSTARD
AND CHARRO BEANS**

**GINGERSNAP ICE CREAM SANDWICHES
WITH CARAMEL DIPPING SAUCE**

SNAKE CREEK GRILL
ONION SOUP

. . . .

1 tablespoon extra virgin olive oil

2 large onions, sliced thin and julienned

1 tablespoon chopped garlic

1 tablespoon chopped shallot

1/2 cup sherry

8 cups chicken stock (Swanson's fat free is
   recommended if homemade not available)

1-1/2 teaspoons kosher salt

1/4 teaspoon white pepper

1/4 cup olive oil, butter, or any fat of choice

1/4 cup flour

Asiago cheese

Chives, chopped

Croutons

Heat olive oil in large pan over medium heat.

Place onions in pan. Slowly let the onions caramelize. (This takes time, about 30 minutes total.) Stir in garlic and shallots, cooking for an additional 2 to 3 minutes.

Deglaze the pan with sherry over high heat and until the liquid is reduced by half (should take less than a minute). Add chicken stock, salt, and pepper. Simmer 40 minutes.

While soup is simmering, make the roux: Pour oil in a small sturdy pan and place it over medium-low heat. When oil is warm, start adding the flour, a teaspoon at a time, stirring continually, until the mixture is thick, about the texture of wet concrete. Add more oil or flour as needed. Stir continually until the flour begins to turn light golden in color.
Set aside.

Place 3 cups stock-onion mixture in blender, add roux, and blend. Return to pot and bring to a boil; turn heat down and simmer 10 minutes more.

Garnish with Asiago cheese, chopped chives, and croutons.

BABY SPINACH SALAD WITH POMEGRANATE SEEDS AND HONEY-BALSAMIC VINAIGRETTE

. . . .

12 cups baby spinach

1 sliced sweet onion, such as Vidalia or Walla Walla

1-1/2 cups Iowa Maytag blue cheese

3/4 cup toasted hazelnuts, skinned if necessary

1-1/2 cups pomegranate seeds

Honey-Balsamic Vinaigrette

Divide spinach between 6 salad plates. Scatter sliced onions over spinach, and then crumble blue cheese on top. Sprinkle hazelnuts and pomegranate seeds across each salad and drizzle with vinaigrette.

HONEY-BALSAMIC VINAIGRETTE

1 cup balsamic vinegar

1/2 teaspoon fresh garlic, minced

1 tablespoon honey

1 tablespoon Dijon mustard

2 cups canola oil

Place vinegar, garlic, honey, and mustard in a blender or food processor and blend until combined. Slowly add oil in a thin stream with blender running until emulsified. Makes 3 cups.

BLUE CORNMEAL CRUSTED RED TROUT WITH TOMATILLO-CHIPOTLE SAUCE AND CHIPOTLE CREMA

. . . .

1 cup blue cornmeal (regular works fine
   but blue adds an interesting color)

1 tablespoon dry mustard

1-1/2 teaspoons whole mustard seed, lightly
   toasted in skillet and finely ground when cool

1-1/2 teaspoons sugar

2 teaspoons coriander

1 teaspoon granulated garlic or
   1/2 teaspoon garlic powder

1 teaspoon salt

1 teaspoon pepper

1/2 teaspoon chile powder

6 trout fillets (6 to 8 ounces each)

2 cups buttermilk

2 tablespoons canola or other oil

Tomatillo-Chipotle Sauce

Chipotle Crema

Cilantro sprigs for garnish

Preheat oven to 400 degrees F.

Thoroughly mix cornmeal, dry mustard, mustard seed, sugar, coriander, garlic, salt, pepper, and chili powder in a bowl. With the skin left on, place the trout fillets in a bowl of buttermilk. Remove fillets one at a time and dredge through the crust mixture. Place fillets in the refrigerator, uncovered, to chill.

Heat a large sauté pan; add oil. Sauté the fillets, flesh side down, until golden brown; turn skin side down and finish in oven for about 5 minutes. Place on plate, skin side down. Spoon on and spread 1-1/2 tablespoons Tomatillo-Chipotle Sauce over the top of the fillet. Drizzle a teaspoon of Chipotle Crema over the tomatillo sauce. Garnish with a sprig of cilantro.

TOMATILLO-CHIPOTLE SAUCE

5 tomatillos

1/2 poblano chile, seeded and coarsely chopped

2 whole garlic cloves

2 cups water

1/2 avocado

1/4 bunch cilantro

Salt and pepper to taste

Place tomatillos, poblano chile, garlic cloves, and water in a small saucepan. Bring to a boil and let simmer at a low boil for about 5 minutes. Remove from heat and let cool. After ingredients have cooled, strain, reserving the water. Place the tomatillo-garlic-chile mixture, along with the avocado and cilantro, in a blender. Slowly add the reserved water until mixture reaches a smooth consistency. Add salt and pepper to taste.

CHIPOTLE CREMA

1/2 cup sour cream

1 chipotle pepper

Up to 2 tablespoons heavy cream

Salt and pepper to taste

In a small food processor, mix the sour cream and chipotle pepper, slowly adding heavy cream a teaspoon at a time until mixture reaches a smooth consistency. Add salt and pepper to taste.

CHILI CORN CUSTARD

. . . .

2 tablespoons butter

3/4 cup whole milk

3/4 cup heavy cream

3 eggs

1 egg yolk

Dash grated nutmeg

2 tablespoons finely diced poblano chile

1/2 cup plus 1 tablespoon corn, fresh or frozen

6 tablespoons grated Monterey Jack cheese

Preheat oven to 325 degrees F.

Melt butter and coat six 3-1/2 to 4 ounce ramekins. Whisk together milk, cream, eggs, egg yolk, and nutmeg. Sprinkle 1 teaspoon diced poblano into each ramekin; add 1-1/2 tablespoons corn and then 1 tablespoon cheese. Fill each ramekin with egg mixture.

Place ramekins in small baking dish and add hot water to dish until it comes 3/4 of the way up the sides of the ramekins. Cover with foil and perforate foil with a knife so steam can escape. Bake 30 minutes; remove foil and continue to cook until top is slightly brown. Custards are done when a knife inserted into the custard comes out clean. Remove from oven and let stand for 5 minutes before serving.

CHARRO BEANS

. . . .

2 tablespoons oil

2 teaspoons minced garlic

2 teaspoons minced shallot

1 tablespoon minced serrano pepper

1/4 cup diced poblano chile

1/4 cup diced red bell pepper

1/4 cup diced yellow bell pepper

1/4 cup diced red onion

2 tablespoons brandy

1-1/2 cups dried pinto beans, precooked (or 2 (15-ounce) cans)

About 1-1/2 cups vegetable stock

1-1/2 teaspoons salt

1-1/2 teaspoons black pepper

1-1/2 teaspoons cumin

1-1/2 teaspoons coriander

1-1/2 teaspoons sugar

1-1/2 teaspoons lime juice

1 teaspoon to 1 tablespoon Tabasco sauce, depending on desired heat

1/4 cup fresh cilantro, chopped

In large pot, sauté garlic, shallots, and minced serrano pepper in oil. Add poblano chile, bell peppers, and onion and sauté until onions are soft.

Deglaze pan with brandy for about 15 seconds, and then add precooked beans. Add vegetable stock until beans are just covered. Add remaining ingredients and simmer for 5 minutes, until stock comes to a boil. Remove from heat and transfer to a ceramic or glass dish.

Refrigerate for 4 hours or overnight. Beans are best when made a day ahead, as flavor improves with age.

GINGERSNAP ICE CREAM SANDWICHES WITH CARAMEL DIPPING SAUCE

. . . .

2 cups plus 2 tablespoons flour

2 teaspoons baking soda

1-1/2 teaspoons salt

1 teaspoon cinnamon

2 teaspoons powdered ginger

1/2 teaspoon powdered cloves

1/4 teaspoon allspice

1/4 teaspoon finely ground pepper

6 ounces (1-1/2 sticks) unsalted butter

1 cup light brown sugar

1 egg

1/4 cup molasses

1 cup milk, for coating

About 1 cup sugar, for coating

**3 to 5 cups vanilla ice cream (about 1/2 to
    3/4 cup per cookie)**

Caramel Sauce (1/4 to 1/2 cup per sandwich)

Sift together first 8 ingredients; set aside. Cream the butter and brown sugar. Mix in the egg and molasses until the mixture is light in color. Slowly add the dry ingredients.

Refrigerate the dough for 30 minutes.

Preheat oven to 375 degrees F.

Roll out dough to 1/4-inch thickness. Cut with large round cookie cutter or small fluted tart shell pan. Brush with milk and sprinkle with sugar. Bake for 12 to 14 minutes. Rotate pan 180 degrees halfway through cooking time. Let cool.

To fill: Let ice cream soften at room temperature for half an hour, and then mix until creamy. Place in piping bag and pipe 1/2 to 3/4 cup onto one gingersnap. Top with a second gingersnap and place in freezer to set. Once set, wrap individually in plastic wrap. Serve on plate with caramel sauce drizzled over top, and, if desired, in small cup to side for dipping. Makes up to 12 sandwiches.

CARAMEL SAUCE

1 cup packed brown sugar

1 cup heavy whipping cream

6-1/2 ounces unsalted butter

In a small saucepan over low heat, combine the sugar, cream, and butter. Stir until the sugar dissolves and the butter melts. Continue to stir for 3 to 5 minutes until warm.

Serve immediately or refrigerate, covered, for up to 2 days. Reheat slowly before serving. Makes 2-1/2 cups.

Snake Creek Grill's
Salmon Cakes with
Cajun Remoulade

WESTERN COMFORT

Traditional western food has always leaned toward the filling, tasty, and satisfying. It's comfort food, ranch-style.

Traditional western hospitality has always been based on two things: feeding a crowd, such as at a barn-raising or a branding; and being prepared to offer a meal to anyone who happened by, no matter the time, weather, or circumstances.

Hearty soups, stews, and casseroles; breads and biscuits warm from the oven; homey, unpretentious desserts—these are the foods that settled the West. And these are the foods (rounded out today with fresh produce and salads, and perhaps a nice bottle of Pinot) that spell home cooking for most westerners. ⫸→

CHICO HOT SPRINGS'
HEIRLOOM BREAD

. . . .

8 cups bread flour

1 tablespoon salt

3 cups warm water (approximately 110 degrees F)

2 tablespoons instant yeast

1/2 cup cornmeal

1 egg white

1/2 teaspoon salt

Place flour, salt, water, and yeast into an electric mixer fitted with a dough hook. (If you are mixing the dough by hand, be sure to use swift, strong strokes to prevent overmixing.) Combine ingredients thoroughly, adding more flour as necessary to achieve a soft, smooth texture. Knead for 10 minutes.

Move dough to a clean bowl (do not coat in oil) and cover with plastic wrap. Let rise until it doubles in size (about 1 to 1-1/2 hours). Gently punch down dough and divide into two equal pieces. Let rest 5 minutes. Flatten each piece into an oval and form into desired shape. Be careful not to knead or handle it too much at this stage because it will become tough. Place on baking sheet sprinkled with cornmeal, or into a French loaf pan. Cover and let rise until the loaves almost double in size (about 30 minutes).

Preheat oven to 425 degrees F. Combine the egg white and salt; brush loaves generously with the mixture. Slash loaves diagonally with a sharp serrated knife in three or four places. Bake for 15 minutes, and then reduce heat to 375 degrees F. Bake 30 minutes more until bread is golden and crusty. Makes 2 loaves.

SWEETWATER'S GREEN
CHILE MAC AND CHEESE

. . . .

2 tablespoons butter

1/2 cup breadcrumbs or panko

1 pint heavy cream

2 tablespoons roasted garlic (approximately 4 to 5 cloves)

1 (2-ounce) can green chiles, drained

3/4 pound Velveeta (Chef Brad Hoch calls it "the miracle cheese")

Salt and pepper to taste

1 (16-ounce) package elbow macaroni

Preheat oven to 350 degrees F.

Melt butter in sauté pan, and then add breadcrumbs or panko and stir until toasted a light golden color. Set aside.

Heat cream, roasted garlic, and green chiles in a heavy medium saucepan. Puree mixture and return to saucepan. Add Velveeta in portions, stirring often. Season with salt and pepper to taste.

While sauce is heating, bring large pot of salted water to boil. Cook pasta in water until al dente, about 8 minutes. Drain.

Combine pasta with sauce in original saucepan and gently mix together until creamy and pasta is coated with sauce. Transfer mixture to ungreased baking dish or casserole. Sprinkle breadcrumbs over top and bake until bubbling on edges, about 15 minutes.

Serve immediately with a green salad and crusty bread. Serves 8.

SNAKE CREEK GRILL'S
SALMON CAKES WITH
CAJUN REMOULADE

• • • • • • • • • • •

SALMON CAKES

1 salmon fillet (16 ounces), skinned, bones removed

3 tablespoons canola oil, divided

1/2 red bell pepper, finely diced

1/2 yellow bell pepper, finely diced

1/2 poblano pepper, finely diced

1 tablespoon lemon juice

1-1/2 tablespoons panko breadcrumbs, divided

1 chipotle pepper, finely diced

1/2 teaspoon salt

1/4 teaspoon pepper

1 egg, beaten

Cajun Remoulade

Grill salmon fillet to medium rare; set aside.

Heat 1 tablespoon canola oil in sauté pan and sauté red bell, yellow bell, and poblano peppers quickly. Transfer to a plate and allow to cool.

Gently tear salmon into small pieces and place in a mixing bowl. Add sautéed peppers, lemon juice, 1 tablespoon panko crumbs, chopped chipotle pepper, salt, and pepper. Pour beaten egg on top and gently fold in. The mixture should be moist.

Using approximately 2 tablespoons of the mixture for each salmon cake, form into small round patties. Place remaining 1/2 tablespoon panko crumbs on small plate and gently pat each side of salmon cake into crumbs. Place on small tray and chill for 2 hours.

Preheat oven to 400 degrees F.

Heat remaining 2 tablespoons canola oil in sauté pan. Sauté a few cakes at a time lightly on each side. Place on an ungreased baking sheet and bake in oven for approximately 3 to 4 minutes. Serve with Cajun Remoulade. Serves 6 as an appetizer or 4 as a main course.

CAJUN REMOULADE

1 red bell pepper, roasted, peeled, and pressed lightly between
**   2 paper towels to remove moisture**

1 egg yolk

1/2 small clove garlic

1-1/2 tablespoons horseradish

1 serrano pepper

1 tablespoon lemon juice

1-1/2 tablespoons capers

1 tablespoon parsley

1-1/2 cups canola oil

Salt and pepper to taste

Place all ingredients except canola oil and salt and pepper in a food processor. While processing, slowly add the canola oil, allowing it to emulsify. Finish with salt and pepper to taste.

BRETECHE CREEK'S PEANUT BUTTER CHOCOLATE CHIP COOKIES

· · · · · · · · · · ·

A staple at the Wyoming educational guest ranch founded and run by the authors.

1 cup unsalted butter, softened

1 cup all-natural peanut butter

1 cup sugar

1 cup brown sugar

2 eggs

1 teaspoon vanilla

2 cups flour

1 teaspoon baking soda

1 teaspoon salt

1 cup semisweet chocolate chips

Preheat oven to 350 degrees F.

Cream butter and peanut butter together until fluffy. Add sugars and blend well. Add eggs, one at a time, and then mix in vanilla.

Mix flour, baking soda, and salt together; add to batter. Mix in chocolate chips.

Use ice-cream scoop to size balls of dough, placing balls about 4 inches apart on ungreased cookie sheets. Wet hand and flatten cookies slightly with palm.

Bake about 14 minutes until golden brown. Let cool on baking sheets until firm. Makes 12 large cookies.

CHICO
HOT
SPRINGS

PRAY, MONTANA

"This is a place built on nostalgia," says writer Seabring Davis of Chico Hot Springs, a legendary resort established more than a century ago during the height of the Montana gold rush. Chico has evolved with the times, starting as a basic boardinghouse offering a hot bath and home-made meal to dust-choked miners, to a twenty-room whiteclapboard inn with fine china, white linen tablecloths, and a hot-spring-fed pool—the height of turn-of-the-century refinement.

When Mike Art happened upon Chico in the 1970s, though, the inn had fallen into disrepair. Art bought it, and with his wife, Eve, began the long process of bringing it back to life. As Eve Art writes in the forward to *A Montana Table,* "Our setting is [at the base of] a spectacular 10,900-foot mountain, with high peaks surrounding the resort on all sides— golden and rosy in the summer and capped by snow sprinkles in the winter, and all this is graced by a natural hot spring that flows through the property."

The hotel's appearance has not changed much over

the years, still a white clapboard, green-trimmed structure in a spectacular setting. Necessary upgrades such as heating and plumbing remain hidden from the eye, while contemporary comforts like the 1998 stone-and-clapboard convention center and a spa offering upscale treatments appear to have always been there.

Today's guests ride and hike in the summer; they experience dog sledding and go cross-country skiing in the winter; year round, they can drive the thirty-five miles to see Yellowstone National Park's spectacular geysers, waterfalls, and wildlife. The nearby Yellowstone River offers fifty miles of whitewater rafting and blue-ribbon trout fishing.

At the end of the day, whether active or indulgent, guests come back to the food. Even in 1900, Chico's cuisine, though mainly meat-and-potatoes based, was unusually focused on freshness. Even in winter, even in the incredibly remote location, the restaurant, thanks to the grace of the hot spring, was able to offer fresh lettuce, vine-ripened tomatoes, and, remarkably, strawberries.

Thirty years ago, when the Arts bought the run-down inn, they made a conscious decision to turn Chico into an upscale dining destination. Today, in addition to fresh ingredients from the geothermal greenhouse, the menu features local beef, farm-raised poultry, wild game, and fresh trout. Dishes such as Wild Mushroom Bisque, Summer Vegetable Medley, Chico's Mixed Grill of antelope and pheasant, and Flathead Cherry Pie draw from the region's bounty and truly speak of the Mountain West.

Chico is both a legend and an institution, its reputation richly deserved. Colin Davis, manager of Chico for more than a decade, notes that Chico hosted seventy-three weddings in 2007 alone. And the staff goes above and beyond when called upon. When forest fires raged nearby in the summer of 2006, for instance, Chico was asked to feed an army of firefighters until the federal program was up and running. "Managers and housekeepers were making nine hundred sandwiches at a time, the breakfast chef would come in at three a.m. and start cooking hundreds of dozens of eggs, and close to a thousand meals were going out the back door between scheduled functions," he recalls. "And I can tell you, it was an honor for us to serve that role."

Davis, who is both an avid cook and an authoritative wine enthusiast, loves his job. "I can't imagine doing anything else," he says. "Because of Chico's history, because of its patina, it has a personality of its own." »→

COLD WEATHER
MENU FROM
CHICO HOT SPRINGS

• • • • • • • • • • •

Serves 6

FENNEL BREADSTICKS

ROASTED RED PEPPER SOUP

FRENCHED PORK CHOP
WITH CORNBREAD STUFFING
AND APPLE CHUTNEY

LEMON PUDDING CAKE
WITH DRIED-CHERRY COMPOTE

FENNEL BREADSTICKS

1/2 cup warm beer

1/2 cup warm water (approximately 110 degrees F)

1-1/2 teaspoons instant yeast

3 cups bread flour

3/4 teaspoon salt

1/2 cup extra virgin olive oil

3 tablespoons fennel seeds

1 egg

1/4 cup heavy whipping cream

Mix beer, warm water, and yeast; let sit until it bubbles, about ten minutes. Add flour, salt, olive oil, and fennel seeds, then combine in the bowl of an electric mixer fitted with a dough hook attachment, or knead by hand until smooth. Do not overmix. If dough is sticky, add more flour. Place in a well-oiled bowl and let dough rise in a warm place until it doubles in size, about one hour.

Preheat oven to 400 degrees F. Prepare a baking sheet by covering it with wax or parchment paper, and then grease with cooking spray. Flatten dough to about one inch thick with a rolling pin, and then cut into 8-inch-long, 1-inch-wide strips. Roll the strips by hand into long, rounded breadsticks; cut in half. Place sticks on baking sheet.

Whisk egg and whipping cream together; use a brush to coat breadsticks with egg wash. Bake for 15 to 20 minutes, or until golden brown. Makes 4 dozen.

ROASTED RED PEPPER SOUP

. . . .

6 to 8 large red bell peppers

2 quarts chicken stock

Canola oil to coat pan

2 large yellow onions, peeled and sliced for sautéing

1 large carrot, rough diced

4 large shallots, rough diced

32 ounces (4 cups) canned tomatoes with juice,
**   or 6 large tomatoes, peeled and seeded**

4 stalks celery, rough diced

2 cloves garlic, rough diced

1 cup sherry, divided

1 cup heavy whipping cream

1/4 teaspoon saffron

Juice of one lemon

1/2 teaspoon hot sauce (optional)

Salt and pepper to taste

1/2 cup grated Parmesan cheese

Roast whole bell peppers over an open flame on a gas-burning grill or stove top; remove from flame when skin is mostly blackened and immerse in an ice bath to remove skin easily. Seed and dice. (Peppers can also be roasted in a 400-degree F oven for 10 to 20 minutes.) Set aside.

In a large soup pot, warm chicken stock on medium high heat until boiling. Add roasted red bell peppers and let simmer.

Heat a saucepan with oil and sauté onion, carrot, shallots, tomatoes, celery, and garlic until browned. Add 1/2 cup sherry to vegetables, deglazing the pan. Stir and combine with hot chicken stock. On medium high heat, allow mixture to reduce by half, about 1-1/2 hours, stirring occasionally.

Puree mixture in a blender or food processor until smooth. Return to soup pot on low heat. Whisk in whipping cream, saffron, lemon juice, remaining 1/2 cup sherry, and the hot sauce, if desired. Add salt and pepper to taste, simmer for 10 minutes, and serve with freshly grated Parmesan cheese.

FRENCHED PORK CHOP WITH CORNBREAD STUFFING AND APPLE CHUTNEY

. . . .

Although especially appealing in the fall, when apples are at their peak, this is a delightful dish year round; in the spring Chico's chef plates it with fresh-picked asparagus from the hot-springs-fed greenhouse.

6 Frenched (bone-in) pork chops (10 ounces each)
Cornbread Stuffing
Apple Chutney

Cut a slit in each pork chop, starting at the base of the bone and cutting lengthwise toward the center of each loin. Place 1/3 cup of prepared stuffing into each chop and grill 6 to 10 minutes on each side until pork is cooked to medium well. (You can also broil the meat for the same amount of time.) Serve with warm Apple Chutney on the side.

CORNBREAD STUFFING

3 slices bacon, chopped
3 stalks celery, diced
1 large carrot, peeled and diced
1 medium white onion, diced
1/2 cup Madeira wine or sherry
1/2 cup heavy whipping cream
1/4 cup dried cranberries
2 tablespoons fresh sage
4 cups chopped Maple Cornbread

Render fat from bacon; add celery, carrot, and onion. Sauté vegetables until soft; add Madeira or sherry, cream, cranberries, sage, and Maple Cornbread. Stir thoroughly until cornbread has soaked up all liquid and mixture sticks together.

MAPLE CORNBREAD

1 cup milk
1 cup buttermilk
4 eggs
1-1/2 cups vegetable oil
1/2 teaspoon maple extract
1-1/2 cups cornmeal
2 cups bread flour
1 tablespoon salt
1 tablespoon baking powder

Preheat oven to 350 degrees F. Spray a 9 x 13-inch baking dish with cooking spray. Combine milk, buttermilk, eggs, oil, and maple extract in a mixing bowl and whisk to combine. Mix together cornmeal, flour, salt, and baking powder and add to batter. Mix only enough to combine; be careful not to overmix. Pour batter into prepared baking dish and bake for 30 minutes or until golden and set.

If serving alone, serve with honey butter: mix 1/2 pound (2 sticks) softened butter with 1/4 cup of honey until creamy.

APPLE CHUTNEY

2 cups apple juice concentrate

2 tablespoons finely chopped ancho chiles

1/2 tablespoon cornstarch

1/2 tablespoon hot water

2 apples (Gala, Granny Smith, or McIntosh),
   peeled and chopped

1/4 cup chopped red onion

1/4 cup seeded, chopped red bell pepper

Bring apple juice concentrate and chiles to a boil. In a separate container, combine cornstarch and hot water. Once apple juice and chiles begin to boil, add cornstarch mixture. Bring back to a boil and remove from heat. Sauté apples, onion, and bell pepper until soft; add apple concentrate sauce and stir. Serve warm.

LEMON PUDDING CAKE WITH DRIED-CHERRY COMPOTE

. . . .

2/3 cup sugar, plus extra for coating ramekins

2 tablespoons plus 1 teaspoon flour

1/4 teaspoon salt

2 tablespoons finely grated lemon zest

3 large eggs, separated, at room temperature

1-1/4 cups buttermilk

1/4 cup freshly squeezed lemon juice

Dried-Cherry Compote

Preheat oven to 325 degrees F. Generously grease bottom and sides of six 4-ounce ramekins with butter. Coat with sugar and tap out excess.

In a large bowl, combine flour, 2/3 cup sugar, salt, and lemon zest with a whisk. In a separate bowl, whisk together egg yolks, buttermilk, and lemon juice until well blended. Pour liquid ingredients into dry ingredients and mix thoroughly. Set aside.

With an electric mixer, whip egg whites on medium speed until soft peaks form. Fold whites into batter in three additions. Using ladle, fill prepared cups almost to the top. Place cups in a baking dish. Pour hot water into pan to cover three quarters of the way up the cups. Bake puddings for 15 minutes. Turn the pan around and bake for another 15 minutes, until puddings have risen and are firm to the touch. Remove cups from water bath and place on rack to cool slightly before serving. Serve with Dried-Cherry Compote.

DRIED-CHERRY COMPOTE

6 ounces dried cherries

1/3 cup pure maple syrup

1/4 cup apple cider

1/4 cup sugar

1 tablespoon pure vanilla extract

In a medium saucepan, combine cherries, maple syrup, apple cider, sugar, and vanilla. Bring to a boil, stirring to dissolve sugar. Reduce heat and simmer about 20 minutes, until cherries have absorbed liquid and puffed up. Let cool. Store compote in an airtight container in refrigerator for up to a week.

WILCOXSON'S ICE CREAM

LIVINGSTON, MONTANA

Y OU WON'T FIND a Web site for Wilcoxson's. When asked for the manager's e-mail address, the receptionist responds, "I wouldn't know that."

Started by Harold and Esther Wilcoxson in 1912, Wilcoxson's was originally a restaurant, candy shop, and ice cream parlor; over time retail operations closed down and the company focused on what it does best: ice cream. Roberta Martin, the office manager (although she wouldn't call herself that), recalls, "I still remember being a kid, seeing the candy . . . It was heaven."

Not much has changed in almost one hundred years. Today, Harold Wilcoxson, son of Carl and Esther, still comes to the plant every day. They still use the original recipes; the ice cream is still made in-house, the old-fashioned way, using the same pasteurization techniques in place since 1912.

Mike, a plant worker (who insisted he was not who

we wanted to talk to), said proudly, "Wilcoxson's is the best ice cream in the country because we use the finest products." Their milk comes from Dairy Gold in Bozeman, their cream from Meadow Gold in Billings. The sugar is Montana beet-sugar from Western Sugar. "We've always used Montana products," Lori, the plant manager, assured us.

Wilcoxson's comes in more than fifty flavors— sold only in Montana and Wyoming—plus ice cream bars and ice cream sandwiches. Flavors range from old-fashioned vanilla and chocolate to the truly decadent. Their best sellers are vanilla and Moose Tracks, a vanilla-based ice cream with a heavy chocolate ribbon and chocolate/peanut-butter cups.

If Wilcoxson's had a motto—which they don't—it might be a saying popular among Montana ranch folk: "If it ain't broke, don't fix it!"

CHICO HOT SPRINGS'
MONTANA MUD PIE

. . . .

**4 cups chocolate cream-filled cookies,
such as Oreos, crushed into crumbs**

5 tablespoons unsalted butter

3 cups coffee ice cream, slightly softened

1 cup crushed toffee

3 cups vanilla ice cream, slightly softened

1-1/2 cups heavy whipping cream

1 pound semisweet chocolate squares

To prepare crust: Lightly spray a 10-inch pie plate (preferably glass) with cooking spray. (A ten-inch springform pan with removable bottom is fine too.)

Combine 3 cups of crushed cookie crumbs with melted butter and press into bottom and sides of pie plate to form crust. Place in freezer until firm, at least 1 hour.

To prepare filling: Create the first layer by placing the slightly soft coffee ice cream into a mixer fitted with a dough hook and mix until smooth but not runny. Or mix by hand until the ice cream is the consistency of a very thick milkshake.

Remove crust from freezer and spread the ice cream onto the crust. Combine the remaining 1 cup cookie crumbs with the crushed toffee. Reserve a handful for later and spread remaining mix on top of the coffee ice cream.

Place pie back in freezer until very firm, at least one hour. Repeat with vanilla ice cream and place back into freezer until very firm, at least 1 hour.

To prepare the chocolate ganache topping: Heat the heavy cream until just boiling and add semisweet chocolate. Remove from heat. Let stand 2 minutes, and then stir until smooth. Remove pie from freezer and spread ganache over ice cream. Sprinkle the reserved cookie-toffee mixture around rim of pie.

Place pie into freezer for 2 hours before serving. Remove pie from freezer 10 minutes before slicing to serve.

LOG
HAVEN
RESTAURANT

SALT LAKE CITY, UTAH

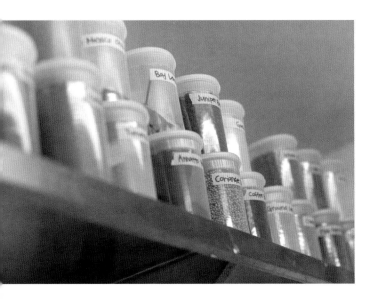

TUCKED UP at the end of a long, narrow canyon and surrounded by Wasatch National Forest, Log Haven is an oasis in the wilderness just half an hour from downtown Salt Lake City. The restaurant is housed in a 1920s log mansion and set on forty scenic acres graced by a duck pond, a waterfall, and fresh-from-the-mountains Mill Creek, which cascades past the restaurant's outdoor patio.

In this unlikely setting—only open for dinner; in winter involving a sometimes white-knuckle drive along curving, iced-over blacktop—steel baron L. H. Rains built an extensive log home as a summer retreat, an anniversary present to his wife. The structure was turned into a year-round residence during the Depression Era, and later became a restaurant before falling into disrepair. Slated for demolition in the 1990s, Log Haven was saved by Margo Provost, a Salt Lake City businesswoman and civic leader who completely restored and refurbished the historic structure. Since then, Log Haven has served sophisticated western fare to thousands of people for après ski and post-hike, for anniversaries and fiftieth birthdays, for business meetings and that special night out—and in keeping with its romantic origins, many, many weddings.

Log Haven's menu changes with the seasons, explains Executive Chef Kevin Donovan, and is locally sourced as much as possible. "I've always been a big fan of supporting local farmers and producers," he says. He seeks out local artisinal products and

forms ongoing relationships with farmers and providers, including fruit growers to the north of Salt Lake and mushroom foragers who comb the Uintas for porcini in the fall.

Donovan, a Business Administration graduate of Creighton University, grew up in St. Louis but "spent as much time in the mountains as I could, in Colorado mostly." His first job, at age sixteen, was

making salads and pizzas at a mom-and-pop pizza shop. His culinary education was on the job. "You learn so much more by working with people; you never have the luxury of making a mistake."

Donovan spent six years cooking in Palm Beach thanks to "a burning desire to cook with seafood and to surf." He surfed every day but eventually, he recalls, "I missed the mountains, the scenery, and the change of seasons." He hung up his board and moved to Utah. Now, when he's not cooking, he can be found in the mountains: snowboarding in the winter, hiking in the summer.

Donovan believes in making everything fresh, from peeling the potatoes by hand each day to his signature ice creams. Of his cuisine, Donovan says, "My food is based on simplicity and balance. The roasted mushrooms are tossed only in a little olive oil, salt and pepper, and that's it. The integrity of the food should come through. I don't like to cover things up. I would rather work with four good ingredients than twelve." ⋙→

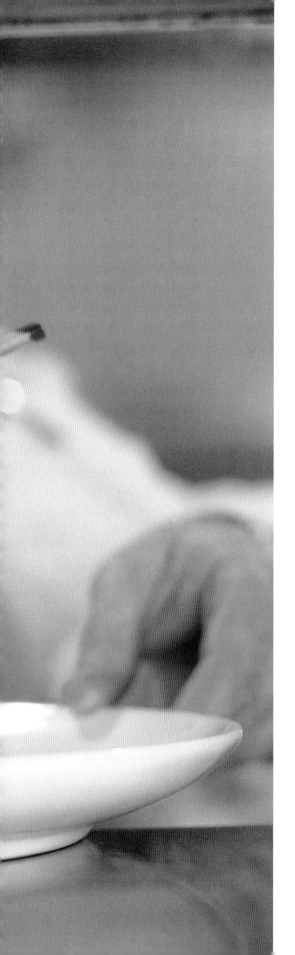

FALL DINNER
IN THE WASATCH
MOUNTAINS

· · · · · · · · · · ·

Serves 6

**CHILLED UTAH HEIRLOOM TOMATO
GAZPACHO WITH CHILE OIL
AND AVOCADO SALSA**

**ROASTED UINTA PORCINI MUSHROOMS
WITH WHITE BEAN PUREE,
PECORINO TOSCANO, AND GRILLED BREAD**

**ROCKY MOUNTAIN ELK CHOP
WITH ARUGULA AND PORCINI JUS,
GOLDEN POTATO HASH,
AND WHOLE ROAST SHALLOTS**

**BEAR LAKE RASPBERRY PUDDING CAKE
WITH GRILLED LEMONS, PORT
BALSAMIC SYRUP, AND HAZELNUT
CRÈME FRAÎCHE ICE CREAM**

CHILLED UTAH HEIRLOOM TOMATO GAZPACHO WITH CHILE OIL AND AVOCADO SALSA

· · · · · · · · · · ·

1 tablespoon olive oil

3 pounds fresh tomatoes, diced

1 cucumber, peeled and diced

1 red onion, diced

2 cloves garlic

1/2 jalapeño pepper, seeds removed and diced

1 cup tomato juice

2 tablespoons lemon juice

1/4 cup sherry vinegar

Salt and pepper to taste

Chile Oil

Avocado Salsa

In a large pot, heat olive oil to medium high heat. Add tomatoes, cucumber, onion, garlic, and jalapeño. Cook for 10 minutes and then remove from heat. Blend mixture in blender until smooth and transfer to large bowl or container. Add tomato juice, lemon, and vinegar, and season with salt and pepper. Allow soup to cool.

Divide soup among 6 bowls. Carefully spoon a generous dollop of Avocado Salsa in the center of each and drizzle Chile Oil across top. Serve room temperature or chilled.

CHILE OIL

1 guajillo chile, or other mild dried chile

1 pint olive oil

Place chile and oil in saucepan; bring to low simmer and remove from heat. Allow chile to steep in oil for 10 minutes. Blend and strain through fine-mesh strainer, and then cool.

AVOCADO SALSA

2 avocados, diced

1/4 cup diced cucumber

2 tablespoons diced red onion

1 roma tomato, diced

1 lime, zested and juiced

1 teaspoon cilantro, chopped

Combine all ingredients in a bowl and mix well. Season with salt and pepper.

ROASTED UINTA PORCINI MUSHROOMS WITH WHITE BEAN PUREE, PECORINO TOSCANO, AND GRILLED BREAD

· · · · · · · · · · ·

1 recipe White Bean Puree

1 recipe Roasted Porcini

3 ounces Pecorino Toscano cheese

6 slices grilled bread

Divided equally between 6 salad plates, mound white bean puree to one side of plate. Arrange porcini over top. Shave Pecorino Toscano over top and lay a slice of grilled bread alongside.

WHITE BEAN PUREE

2 cups dried white beans

2 pieces bacon

2 bay leaves

2 quarts water

Salt and pepper to taste

Soak beans in water overnight in refrigerator. Drain beans and place in pot with bacon and bay leaves; cover with water by 2 inches. Cover and bring to a boil; cook beans for 45 to 60 minutes until tender.

Strain beans, reserving liquid. Remove bacon and bay leaves. Place beans in a blender or food processor and blend until smooth, adding liquid until desired consistency is achieved. Season with salt and pepper.

ROASTED PORCINI

8 ounces fresh porcini mushrooms

3 tablespoons olive oil

Salt and pepper to taste

Preheat oven to 450 degrees F. Slice porcini in half lengthwise, toss with olive oil, and place on a baking sheet. Season with salt and pepper and roast in oven for 6 to 8 minutes.

ROCKY MOUNTAIN ELK CHOP WITH ARUGULA AND PORCINI JUS

· · · · · · · · · · ·

**6 elk chops (may substitute beef rib-eye steak,
about 2" thick)**
1/4 cup olive oil
2 tablespoons salt
2 tablespoons pepper
Porcini Jus
12 large arugula leaves

Simply rub a touch of your favorite olive oil on the elk chop
or steak. Season with salt and fresh cracked black pepper
and grill to medium rare, about 4 to 5 minutes per side,
depending on the thickness of the chop.

To assemble dish, divide porcini jus among plates, allowing it
to spread thinly from center. Place one scoop of potato
hash slightly off center on each plate. Divide whole shallots
among plates, clustering them next to potato mounds. Prop
the meat up against the mound of hash and garnish the dish
with fresh arugula leaves.

PORCINI JUS

1/2 ounce dried porcini mushrooms
1/2 quart warm water
Salt and pepper

Soak porcini in water and let sit for 20 minutes. Transfer to
blender and blend until smooth. Transfer to small saucepan
and heat gently until warm. Season with salt and pepper.

GOLDEN POTATO HASH

· · · · · · · · · · ·

Pinch of saffron
2 pounds Yukon gold potatoes, 1/4 inch diced
1/2 pound bacon, diced
1 leek, diced
1 tablespoon chopped fresh sage
Salt and pepper

Bring enough water to boil to hold the potatoes. When
water is boiling, add the saffron and then the potatoes and
cook for 10 minutes. Strain the potatoes and set aside.
Meanwhile, heat sauté pan and cook bacon until golden
brown. Add leek and sage and cook for 2 more minutes,
and then remove from heat. Combine potatoes and bacon
mixture and toss to combine. Season with salt and pepper.

WHOLE ROAST SHALLOTS

· · · · · · · · · · ·

2 pounds whole shallots, peeled
1/2 cup olive oil
1 tablespoon thyme

Preheat oven to 400 degrees F. Place shallots, olive oil,
and thyme in ovenproof dish. Cover with foil and roast in
oven for 1 hour.

BEAR LAKE RASPBERRY PUDDING CAKE WITH GRILLED LEMON, PORT BALSAMIC SYRUP, AND HAZELNUT CRÈME FRAÎCHE ICE CREAM

. . . .

PUDDING CAKES

1/2 cup plus 1 tablespoon sugar, plus extra for coating
   insides of ramekins

3 cups fresh raspberries

6 tablespoons unsalted butter, cubed

3 eggs, separated

2 tablespoons flour

1/4 cup plus 2 tablespoons milk

3 tablespoons lemon juice

Pinch cream of tartar

Grilled Lemon Segments

Port Balsamic Syrup

Hazelnut Crème Fraîche Ice Cream

Fresh raspberries for garnish

Preheat oven to 325 degrees F.

Butter the bottom and insides of six 6-ounce ramekins.
Sprinkle sugar inside and swirl to coat.

Puree the berries in a food processor and strain through a
fine-mesh sieve. Measure 3/4 cup puree and reserve the
remainder for another use. Stir berry puree and butter over
double boiler until butter is melted. Stir in lemon juice.
Mix egg yolks and 6 tablespoons sugar in separate bowl until
lighter in color. Gradually add warm berry mixture while
stirring. Return bowl to double boiler.

Cook, whisking constantly, until curd reaches 160 degrees F. Remove from heat and stir in flour and then milk.

Using a mixer, whip egg whites and cream of tartar until foamy. Add remaining 3 tablespoons sugar gradually while continually whipping, until the whites hold stiff peaks. Carefully fold whipped whites into curd.

Divide mixture between buttered and sugared ramekins. Place ramekins in large baking dish and pour hot water halfway up sides to create a water bath. Bake for 20 to 30 minutes until set; should be firm to the touch.

To assemble dessert, unmold raspberry pudding cake onto small pool of balsamic syrup; can pool or streak another teaspoon of sauce across plate. Place small scoop of Hazelnut Crème Fraîche Ice Cream to side of plate, with several Grilled Lemon Segments at top of plate. Garnish with fresh raspberries.

HAZELNUT CRÈME FRAÎCHE ICE CREAM

3 cups milk

1-1/2 cups hazelnuts, toasted and finely ground

1 vanilla bean, scraped

12 egg yolks

1-1/4 cups sugar

3 cups crème fraîche

1 tablespoon Frangelico

In a saucepan, bring the milk to a simmer. Add ground hazelnuts and vanilla bean. Infuse in refrigerator overnight. Strain.

Scald the infused milk in a saucepan. Whisk the egg yolks and sugar in a bowl. Gradually whisk in the hot milk. Return

mixture to the saucepan and stir over medium heat until custard thickens and leaves a path on the back of the spoon when you draw your finger across (about 160 degrees F). Do not let the mixture boil. Transfer mixture to a container and add crème fraîche and Frangelico. Chill. Churn in an ice cream maker according to manufacturer's directions. Makes about 3 quarts.

GRILLED LEMON SEGMENTS

3 cups sugar

3/4 cup water

3 slices fresh ginger (1/4-inch thick each)

1/4 cup plus 2 tablespoons rum

1/2 vanilla bean, scraped

4 lemons, segmented

Bring sugar, water, and ginger to a boil. Transfer to storage container and add rum, vanilla bean, and lemon segments. Let rest overnight in the refrigerator.

Grill segments until caramelized around edges and grill marks appear.

PORT BALSAMIC SYRUP

3/4 cup port

1/4 cup brown sugar

1/2 cup balsamic vinegar

Simmer until reduced by half. Makes about 3/4 cup.

VINTAGE
RESTAURANT

KETCHUM, IDAHO

V INTAGE RESTAURANT in wintertime is the quintessence of rustic mountain charm. A brown picket fence entwined with small white lights and draped with snow gives way to a wooden gate with a handcarved sign overhead: "Vintage" silhouetted against local landmark Baldy Mountain.

A wooden boardwalk winds between mounds of snow to the front door of a 1927 log cabin. The door opens to a mellow white-tableclothed, glowing-wood-walled warmth, where good food and good conversation reign in a convivial atmosphere orchestrated by veteran chef, cookbook author, and owner Jeff Keys.

Like many people in Sun Valley, Keys is "from away." Keys spent his childhood in southern California, where there was an abundance of fresh local fruit, vegetables, and fish. In terms of food, he was influenced by his grandparents, who tended chickens, a vegetable garden, and avocado and citrus trees; they also hunted and fished. Every meal was fresh and local. As a youth, he was always drawn to the mountains. Skipping southern

California's beach scene, Keys would drive seven hundred miles round-trip to ski at Mammoth Mountain. When he returned, he recalls, "I would be filled up with the energy of the mountains."

As a teenager, inspired by an article on Colorado in *Arizona Highways* magazine, he packed his VW bug and, with one hundred dollars, set off for Aspen. Over the next twenty years Keys became a cook, starting as a ski bum/lowly dishwasher and eventually falling by accident into cooking. Over time he became a bona fide chef, learning all the way—a process that he says still continues today, even after all those years at the range.

Vintage is a "unique, untamed little restaurant, a microwild area in the middle of a modern mountain town," he says. "At Vintage we don't overwork or over-stylize our food or our atmosphere. We are naturally elegant, rustic, warm, and friendly. We do as little handling of the food as possible. We let the natural beauty and intrinsic value of the ingredients tell us what to do."

Vintage recipes are energetic. Starters should "wake up your taste buds, stimulate your appetite, and get you excited about the coming meal," Keys says. His offerings include a Prawn and Goat Cheese Tart, Seared Flatiron Steak Satay, and Smoked Wild King Salmon Pâté. Salads—"a little thunder and lightning before the rain"—range from an Heirloom Tomato Bread Salad to a Warm Fingerling Potato Salad. Chef Keys loves a good soup: Baked Onion and Roasted Tomato; Leek, Brie, and Yukon Gold Potato Chowder; and Avocado Gazpacho. Entrees showcase the regional and fresh, and include Crispy Skin Roast Duck, Idaho Rib-Eye Steak, Pecan Crusted Chicken, and Applewood Smoked Pork Loin Chop with Gorgonzola Polenta and Caramelized Yams. Keys is passionate about dessert and features homemade ice cream on his menu every day, as well as such inspirations as Chocolate Chunk Bread Pudding with Whiskey Sabayon Sauce, Blood Orange Crème Brûlée, and Frozen Key Lime Soufflé.

Keys embraces culinary techniques from around the world, yet uses as many local and seasonal ingredients as possible: mountain berries, local grass-fed lamb, even fresh produce from his home garden at his farm south of Sun Valley. "I used to grow lots of produce for the restaurant," he says, "but as my family grew and the business took off, I now rely on as many local growers and gardeners as I can find: Laura Sluder of Blue Sage Farms out of Shoshone for lamb; Judith Walker up East Fork for baby greens and fresh herbs; Tommy Malaine out of Hagerman for all things produce, including some of the best tomatoes in the world; Atkinson's Valley Market for all kinds of great produce, organic grains and organic flour, and naturally raised beef and pork from Idaho and Oregon; Stuart Siderman for the freshest fish this side of Seattle; and lots of very kind gardeners who just bring us their products when they are perfectly ready." For this chef, it's all about showcasing the best of his little corner of the still-wild Mountain West. ⟫→

SUN VALLEY WARM
WINTER MENU

· · · · · · · · · · · ·

Serves 6

**BIBB LETTUCE SALAD WITH PEARS,
GORGONZOLA, AND ORANGE-PECAN DRESSING**

**HAGERMAN BUTTERNUT SQUASH SOUP,
SZECHUAN STYLE**

**BUTTERFLIED LEG OF LAMB, GRILLED
MUSHROOM AND SWEET ONION RELISH, AND
RED WINE AND FRESH SAGE DRIZZLE, WITH
TWICE-BAKED POTATOES**

**VINTAGE SIGNATURE CHOCOLATE
TRUFFLE TORTE**

BIBB LETTUCE SALAD WITH PEARS, GORGONZOLA, AND ORANGE-PECAN DRESSING

. . . .

Generous squeeze of half a lemon

2 fresh pears, peeled, cored, and thinly sliced

6 handfuls torn Bibb lettuce, cleaned and dried

6 ounces Gorgonzola cheese, crumbled

8 to 10 tablespoons Orange-Pecan Dressing

Squeeze lemon juice over pear slices. Place lettuce in a salad bowl with Gorgonzola and dressing and toss lightly. Pile the salad onto 6 chilled plates. Fan one half of each sliced pear over each salad and drizzle a little more dressing over the top before serving.

ORANGE-PECAN DRESSING

3 tablespoons seasoned rice vinegar

1/3 cup honey (chef likes orange blossom honey for this dressing)

1 teaspoon freshly grated orange zest

3 tablespoons fresh orange juice

1/2 cup olive oil or vegetable oil

1/4 cup pecans, toasted and chopped

Put rice vinegar, honey, orange zest, orange juice, and oil in a mixing bowl and whip with a wire whisk until honey has dissolved and blended with other ingredients. Add pecans. This dressing will keep for 2 to 3 weeks in the refrigerator.

HAGERMAN BUTTERNUT SQUASH SOUP, SZECHUAN STYLE

. . . .

1 medium yellow onion, diced

1 fennel bulb, diced

2 cloves garlic, diced

20 ounces butternut squash, peeled and cut into
chunks (approximately 1 large squash)

2 tablespoons ginger, peeled and thinly sliced

1-1/2 tablespoons vegetable oil

1 quart chicken or vegetable stock

1/8 teaspoon red chile flakes (optional)

1 teaspoon Asian chile sauce (such as Sriracha,
found at most supermarkets)

1 cup Thai coconut milk

2 tablespoons Vintage Basic Asian Marinade

2 tablespoons creamy peanut butter

1 teaspoon toasted sesame oil

1/2 cup cream

Sauté the onion, fennel, garlic, squash, and ginger with the vegetable oil in a small soup pot for about 5 minutes on medium low heat, stirring frequently. Add stock, chile flakes, and Asian chile sauce. Cook on low boil for about 35 minutes or until vegetables are soft. Add coconut milk and cook for 5 additional minutes. Add remaining ingredients and remove from heat. Let the soup cool, and then puree in batches in a blender. At this point the soup can be reheated and served, or cooled further and stored for several days in the refrigerator.

Serving suggestion: Serve garnished with pickled ginger and freshly snipped basil, or with thin slices of grilled Muscovy duck breast and sliced green onions.

VINTAGE BASIC ASIAN MARINADE

Chef Keys uses this to marinate fish, lamb, pork, or chicken before grilling. It's also great as a base for other Asian marinades and for drizzling over meat or fish after cooking.

2 cups soy sauce

3/4 cup brown sugar

1 tablespoon plus one teaspoon coarse ground
black pepper

2 teaspoons whole fennel seeds

10 cloves garlic, diced

1 tablespoon fresh grated ginger

Mix all ingredients in a bowl.

Note: This marinade is very potent and will absorb quickly into meat. If marinating fish, do not let it rest in the marinade; just put it in then take it out. For chicken breasts and pork, let marinate about 5 minutes. For butterflied leg of lamb, about 15 minutes. The marinade will store in the refrigerator for up to 10 days.

BUTTERFLIED LEG OF LAMB WITH GRILLED MUSHROOM AND SWEET ONION RELISH AND RED WINE AND FRESH SAGE DRIZZLE

. . . .

Chef Keys loves serving Idaho-raised lamb. "It captures the flavor of the region: The infinite sunlight, the aroma of the wild sage covering the dry hills, the ever-present western breezes that spread the scent that is literally absorbed by the livestock. It is the taste of the West." Blue Sage Farms is located between Shoshone and Gooding, Idaho, part of a new sensibility springing up in the West that is helping to bring new life and energy to western agriculture.

6 portions butterflied leg of lamb (6 ounces each)
Moose Drool Dark Beer Marinade
Grilled Mushroom and Sweet Onion Relish
Red Wine and Fresh Sage Drizzle
Fresh sage for garnish

Place lamb portions in marinade, and marinate the meat for about 1 hour.

Fifteen minutes before serving, place the twice-baked potatoes in a 375-degree F oven. Begin cooking the lamb on a preheated grill (or under the broiler), turning the portions 2 or 3 times. It will take about 12 minutes to cook the lamb to medium rare. While the lamb is cooking, prepare the Mushroom and Sweet Onion Relish and the Red Wine Drizzle.

When the lamb is finished cooking, remove to a cutting board and let rest for a few minutes. This will allow the meat to relax and it will slice more easily.

To plate the dish, lay out 6 warm dinner plates and place a hot twice-baked potato (see recipe, page 199) at the top of each plate. Spoon some Red Wine Drizzle around the lower half of the plate. Slice each piece of lamb across the grain at a diagonal into 4 or 5 slices and fan them out over the wine drizzle. Spoon an equal portion of the relish over the lamb. Garnish each plate with a sprig of fresh sage.

MOOSE DROOL DARK BEER MARINADE

1 12-ounce bottle Moose Drool or other dark beer
1/4 cup dark brown sugar
2 teaspoons Vintage Restaurant Spice Mix,
**   or 1 teaspoon salt and 1 teaspoon pepper**

Blend mixture well until sugar dissolves.

VINTAGE RESTAURANT'S SPICE MIX

Use for roasts, in barbecue spice rubs, and in barbecue sauces.

2 tablespoons mild chile powder

I tablespoon Spanish paprika

I tablespoon fresh ground black pepper

I tablespoon Kosher salt

I tablespoon ground toasted cumin seed

I tablespoon whole fennel seeds

I tablespoon curry powder

I tablespoon dry whole-leaf thyme

I tablespoon cayenne pepper

I tablespoon onion powder

I tablespoon granulated garlic

Mix all ingredients together and store in a tightly covered container. The spice mix is at its best for thirty days.

GRILLED MUSHROOM AND SWEET ONION RELISH

6-1/4-inch thick slices of sweet red or yellow onions

Approx. 1/4 cup plus I tablespoon extra virgin olive oil, divided

24 medium-sized cremini mushrooms, or other mushrooms

2 tablespoons freshly snipped basil leaves

2 tablespoons thinly sliced green onion

Pinch kosher salt

Pinch freshly ground pepper

I tablespoon balsamic vinegar

Brush both sides of the onion slices with approximately 2 tablespoons olive oil. Cut the mushrooms in half and put them into a mixing bowl; drizzle with approximately 2 more tablespoons olive oil. While the lamb portions are cooking, spread out the mushrooms and onion slices on a grill or on a baking sheet under the broiler; cook for 2 minutes. Turn the vegetables over and cook for 2 more minutes. Remove to a mixing bowl, add the remaining ingredients, and toss with balsamic vinegar and remaining I tablespoon olive oil.

RED WINE AND FRESH SAGE DRIZZLE

1/2 teaspoon olive oil

2 tablespoons finely diced sweet onion

1/2 cup hearty red wine

1/8 teaspoon freshly ground pepper

12 fresh sage leaves

I teaspoon French Dijon mustard

1-1/2 tablespoons cold unsalted butter

Heat a 6-inch stainless steel sauté pan. Add the olive oil and diced onions and sauté until the onions turn translucent, about 2 minutes. Add wine, ground pepper, and sage leaves and simmer until it reduces its volume by half. Whisk in the mustard, lower the heat, and whisk in the butter until thoroughly blended in.

TWICE-BAKED IDAHO RUSSET POTATOES

. . . .

You can vary this recipe very easily by using different cheeses in the mixture, such as Gorgonzola.

4 medium to large Idaho baking potatoes

2 ounces unsalted butter

1 tablespoon extra virgin olive oil

1/4 teaspoon kosher salt

1/4 teaspoon freshly ground pepper

2 ounces sour cream

1 cup grated medium sharp cheddar cheese, divided

1 tablespoon chopped fresh parsley

2 tablespoons chopped green onion

1 tablespoon prepared horseradish (optional)

3 ounces cream cheese, cut into 1/4-inch pieces

Preheat oven to 375 degrees F.

To prepare the twice-bakers, poke each potato with a fork 3 or 4 times. This helps the potato release its inner heat while cooking and keeps it from exploding. Bake the potatoes for about 1 hour and 15 minutes, or until the potatoes are fork tender. Remove the potatoes from the oven and place on a cutting board. While the potatoes are still hot, cut them in half and scoop out the potato pulp into a mixing bowl. Add the butter, olive oil, salt, pepper, sour cream, 1/2 cup cheddar cheese, parsley, green onion, and horseradish (if desired), and blend together just until mixed. Do not over-blend the mixture; it should have a fluffy quality. Fold in the cream cheese.

Save the six neatest halved potato skins and fill each of them with equal portions of the potato mixture, allowing it to mound in the middle. Sprinkle the potatoes with the remaining grated cheese.

Place on a baking sheet and bake for 15 minutes.

VINTAGE SIGNATURE CHOCOLATE TRUFFLE TORTE

. . . .

At Vintage, Chef Keys serves a one-inch wide slice of this torte on a plate decorated with small pools of chocolate sauce and caramel sauce; he places a scoop of homemade ice cream alongside and garnishes with a tablespoon of Bachelor's Berries (berries that have been macerated with sugar and brandy) with their juices.

FOR THE TORTE CRUST:

1 cup lightly toasted pecans

1/2 cup sugar

4-1/2 tablespoons unsalted butter, melted

FOR THE CHOCOLATE TRUFFLE FILLING:

2-1/2 cups good quality semisweet chocolate,
    cut into pieces

1/2 cup unsalted butter, cut into pieces

2 cups heavy cream

6 tablespoons sugar

Pinch of salt

6 tablespoons brandy

Preheat oven to 350 degrees F.

To make the crust, place the pecans and sugar in a food processor; process for a few seconds. Add the butter and process again until evenly blended. Press mixture into the bottom and 1/4 inch up the sides of a 10-inch springform pan. Bake the crust for about 12 minutes, until lightly browned and fragrant. Set aside to cool.

To make the filling, place the chocolate and the butter in a stainless steel bowl over a simmering pot of water. Let the chocolate melt slowly with the butter, stirring until well blended. Remove the bowl from the heat. Meanwhile, put the cream, sugar, and pinch of salt into a saucepan and heat mixture just to the boiling point, stirring to dissolve sugar. Turn off the heat and after letting it cool briefly, add the brandy. Turn the heat back on and bring the mixture back to just boiling. Do not let it boil for longer than a few seconds. Remove from heat immediately.

Pour the cream mixture into the chocolate mixture and blend thoroughly until it is perfectly smooth. Pour the truffle mixture into the pecan crust. Put the torte into the refrigerator for at least 4 hours until firm. Remove the torte from the refrigerator about an hour before serving and unmold.

LAVA LAKE LAMB

THE TENS OF THOUSANDS of pioneers who made the arduous journey over the Goodale's Cutoff of the Oregon Trail would easily recognize the lunar landscape, fringed by mountains, of what is now Craters of the Moon National Monument. After skirting their way around the lava flows, the first natural resting place the pioneers came to—the confluence of several small streams feeding a small lake dammed by the lava—looks much the same today as it did in the 1840s.

What they would not recognize is Lava Lake Lamb's approach to predator management. When wolves threaten the ranch's six thousand hormone- and antibiotic-free, grass-fed ewes and lambs, the herders don't reach for their rifles. Instead they move closer to their bands, sleeping out in the open in high mountain meadows rather than in the comfort of their base camp, and rely on their dogs—huge, loud Great Pyrenees and Akbash guard dogs—to warn of trouble.

When wolves do come, the dogs bark and the herders rouse to frighten the wolves away by shouting and firing loud cracker shells in the air. Usually one walking tour of the sheep band by the herder is all that's necessary; then he can return to bed for a quiet night's sleep.

All is not quiet back at the office, though. Demand for Lava Lake Lamb is brisk and the ranch is also engaged in an array of scientific and conservation projects. "The ranch is 24,000 acres with 850,000 acres of grazing permits. Sixty thousand of those acres are certified organic, with 7,200 acres protected by a perpetual conservation easement held by The Nature Conservancy," says Lava Lake's president, Mike Stevens. "The ranch extends from high desert at four thousand feet to high peaks at almost twelve thousand feet; it's a really dramatic and diverse desert and mountain landscape with lots of charismatic wildlife, from pronghorn antelope to black bears to mountain lions."

And the lamb? It's delicious—tender, and flavored by wild grasses and herbs. It's also healthier than conventionally raised lamb: rich in omega-3 fatty acids, vitamin E, and beta carotene, and lower in fat than grain-fed meat. Lava Lake Lamb ships all over the country and sells directly to discerning chefs in the northern Rockies and at Sun Valley's summertime farmers' market. All net proceeds from their lamb sales are applied to Lava Lake's conservation and habitat-restoration programs in south-central Idaho.

It may not always be easy scaring off wolves and ridding the land of nonnative weeds without pesticides, but at Lava Lake they believe it's worth the effort.

"Philosophically, we believe that the best conservation occurs at the scale of entire landscapes, and we believe predators have a role to play. It's our job to try to coexist with them," says Stevens. "Practically, people want us to be good stewards. That means maintaining an ecologically appropriate level of grazing, restoring streams and other key habitats, and being predator-friendly." ⋙→

2 pounds lamb stew meat
1-1/2 teaspoons sugar
1 tablespoon canola or vegetable oil
1/2 teaspoon salt
1/8 teaspoon pepper
1-1/2 tablespoons flour
1 to 1-1/2 cups beef stock or water
1/2 cup dry white wine
2 cloves garlic, mashed
Bouquet garni: 1 bay leaf, a few parsley sprigs, thyme leaves, celery leaves, and a 2" x 1" piece of orange peel, tied together
3 carrots, cut into 1-1/2" lengths
3 turnips, cut into cubes
6 to 9 pearl onions, peeled
1/4 cup freshly squeezed orange juice
1 tablespoon lemon juice
10 peeled orange sections, preferably from bitter oranges
Chopped parsley

Preheat oven to 350 degrees F. Pat lamb pieces dry, sprinkle with sugar, and brown in oil in skillet over moderately high heat for about 3 minutes. Transfer to an ovenproof casserole. Sprinkle with salt, pepper, and flour. Place casserole in oven for about 6 minutes, stirring lamb twice. Add beef stock, wine, garlic, and bouquet garni. Cover and place in oven, leaving stew to simmer for an hour.

Add vegetables, orange and lemon juices, and more liquid, if needed, so meat and vegetables are just covered. Continue cooking for another hour or until the meat and vegetables are tender. Add orange sections and allow to heat through. Dust with freshly chopped parsley. Serve with crusty bread and a crisp salad. Serves 6 to 8.

SWEETWATER
RESTAURANT

JACKSON, WYOMING

WESTERN ATMOSPHERE in a white-tablecloth restaurant" is how one online reviewer describes Sweetwater Restaurant in Jackson, Wyoming. Located just off the town square, the restaurant—a Jackson institution for thirty years—resides in the historic Coe Cabin, built in 1915 and recognized by the Teton County Historic Preservation Board. One of the oldest buildings in Jackson, the structure—with its boardwalk entry, glowing wood walls, lace curtains, wood stove, and miscellaneous antiques—exudes atmosphere without trying. The feeling is refined but relaxed, the food upscale but unpretentious—"really sophisticated comfort food," is how Head Chef and Partner Trey Davis puts it.

Longtime owner Brad Hoch, a graduate of the California Culinary Academy, started cooking at Sweetwater in 1979; Steve Elvemeyer joined in 1980. Together they bought the restaurant in 1984, and together they plated meals for locals and tourists alike through four seasons a year, even remaining open through "mud season," through the decades, through winter blizzards and Fourth of July crowds. Thirty years is a long time to work a job with five a.m. starts, standing all day, maintaining a constant dance of sorts as the orders come in, get cooked and plated, go out. Brad and Steve brought in Davis as their partner in 2002; he's now in the process of transitioning to sole owner so his partners can finally put their feet up.

Davis, a native of southern Louisiana, grew up cooking on the bayous. "All men there cook," he explains. He attended culinary school at CIA-Louisiana and worked in large hotel kitchens at the Orient Express Hotel in Vail (three years), the Phoenician in Scottsdale (four years), and the Arizona Biltmore Restaurant and Spa (four years). An enthusiastic skier and fly-fisherman, he'd been visiting Jackson regularly for five years when he heard about an opportunity to join as chef and ultimately partner at Sweetwater. The timing was right, Davis recalls. "I'd had as many as 150 chefs working under me. I was tired of hotels and the politics. I never got

to cook; I always had to be out front. I supervised a $40 million food and beverage budget. Now I get to cook, I meet a lot of people; it's a much smaller town. It's fabulous here. I've lived all over the country and this is my favorite place—except," he adds, "southern Louisiana."

Davis follows Hoch's lead in producing comfort food, "and it's going to have southern influences here

and there." At lunchtime there are plenty of fresh salad options, including blackened salmon and Baja chicken, sandwiches, wraps, pork barbecue on a bun, and an elk burger. Dinner offerings change seasonally and include baked Brie and chile-lime crab cakes for starters, and entrees such as elk fettucine, blackened prime rib, lamb chops, and slow-roasted rack of pork. Wintertime might find lamb stew and buffalo pot roast on the menu, summer a pesto-crusted halibut. Vegetarian choices hint at Hoch's interest in Mediterranean cuisine, and desserts are plentiful, housemade, and luscious, such as Sweetwater's signature bread pudding, served in fifteen variations ranging from homey cinnamon-raisin to decadent white chocolate-raspberry.

At Sweetwater the pace is always busy. But it does change with the seasons. "During the winter, ninety percent of our business is locals," says Davis. "In the summer, ninety percent of our business is tourists." ⫸→

· · · · · · · · · · · ·

Serves 6

**CHILE-LIME CRAB CAKES WITH CORN
AND BLACK BEAN RELISH
AND AVOCADO AIOLI**

**TEQUILA-GLAZED SALMON
WITH PICO DE GALLO
AND RED PEPPER GRITS**

CHOCOLATE-TOFFEE BREAD PUDDING

CHILE-LIME CRAB CAKES WITH CORN AND BLACK BEAN RELISH AND AVOCADO AIOLI

. . . .

CRAB CAKES

2 (6-ounce) cans crabmeat (or 12 ounces fresh)

5 green onions, finely chopped

1/2 bunch parsley, finely chopped

1/2 medium yellow onion, finely chopped

1 tablespoon chile paste

2 cups bread crumbs, plus 1 cup for coating

Juice and zest of 1 lime

1/4 cup cilantro, finely chopped

2 eggs

2 tablespoons mayonnaise

2 tablespoons each oil and butter, for frying

Corn and Black Bean Relish

Avocado Aioli

Fresh cilantro and lime wedges for garnish

Combine crabmeat, green onions, parsley, onion, chile paste, bread crumbs, lime juice and zest, cilantro, eggs, and mayonnaise and mix well. Chill mixture at least one hour. Form cakes in desired size. Coat in additional bread crumbs. Brown on both sides in a mixture of oil and butter or clarified butter.

Serve with Corn and Black Bean Relish and Avocado Aioli, and garnish with fresh cilantro and a wedge of lime.

CORN AND BLACK BEAN RELISH

1 tablespoon vegetable oil

1 red onion, diced

1 red bell pepper, diced

2 stalks celery, diced

2 cups corn, fresh or frozen

1 can black beans, drained and rinsed

1 tablespoon cumin

2 tablespoons white wine vinegar

1/2 bunch cilantro, chopped

Salt and pepper to taste

Sauté in oil the onion, bell pepper, and celery until soft. Add corn and black beans for one minute. Add remaining ingredients and mix together. Remove from heat and let cool.

AVOCADO AIOLI

1 avocado, mashed

1 tablespoon lime juice

1/4 cup mayonnaise

Mix ingredients well and serve.

TEQUILA-GLAZED SALMON WITH PICO DE GALLO AND RED PEPPER GRITS

. . . .

This salmon is also delicious when paired with simply prepared potatoes. Sweetwater uses the freshest Idaho potatoes from right over the pass, only about 15 miles away. The chef tosses the potatoes with butter, salt, pepper, and cilantro, then roasts them in a 400-degree F oven for 45 minutes.

6 salmon filets (8 ounces each)
Tequila Glaze
Red Pepper Grits
Pico de Gallo
6 ounces tequila

Preheat oven to 450 degrees F.

Grill salmon on flesh side and place in oven pan. (Or skip the grilling and start in the oven.) Spoon or brush on glaze with a pastry brush. Place salmon in preheated oven and finish cooking for approximately 15 minutes.

To serve, place salmon atop grits and arrange 2 generous spoonfuls of Pico de Gallo over top. Serve with a shot of tequila on plate.

TEQUILA GLAZE

I cup tequila
1/2 cup honey
1/4 cup lime juice

Mix all ingredients in saucepan and cook slowly until reduced by half, about 15 minutes. Let cool slightly until mixture thickens.

PICO DE GALLO

5 tomatoes, diced
1/2 red onion, diced
1/2 jalapeño, minced
1/2 bunch cilantro
Salt and pepper to taste

Gently mix all ingredients in a bowl until combined.

RED PEPPER GRITS

2 cups milk
6 cups chicken stock
5 roasted red bell peppers
2-1/2 cups grits (polenta)
1/2 cup Monterey Jack cheese, grated
Salt and pepper to taste

In a blender, puree milk, stock, and bell peppers until smooth. Transfer to a stockpot and bring to a boil. Slowly whisk in grits and bring back to a boil. Turn to low and simmer about 20 minutes, whisking often until soft. Whisk in cheese and add salt and pepper to taste.

CHOCOLATE-TOFFEE
BREAD PUDDING

. . . .

3 to 5 cups diced bread, stale or fresh toasted,
    cut into one-inch cubes
1 cup semisweet chocolate chips
1 cup toffee bits (or English toffee candy,
    cut into pieces)
1/2 cup sugar
1/3 cup flour
1/2 teaspoon vanilla
4 eggs
3 cups heavy cream or half-and-half
Chocolate shavings or chopped toffee bar (optional)

Preheat oven to 350 degrees F.

Lightly butter a 6-cup baking dish or bread pan. Evenly spread bread cubes in prepared dish. Sprinkle chocolate and toffee bits across top and mix in slightly.

Combine sugar and flour and mix well. Beat in vanilla, eggs, and cream or half-and-half. Pour over mixture in baking dish.

Set dish inside a larger dish and pour boiling water halfway up sides. Carefully place in preheated oven. Bake for about 45 minutes until pudding is set. Serve warm.

Garnish with chocolate shavings or a chopped toffee bar, if desired.

BREAD PUDDING VARIATIONS:

Cinnamon-Raisin:
Substitute chocolate and toffee with 1 cup raisins tossed with 1 teaspoon cinnamon.

White Chocolate-Raspberry:
Substitute chocolate and toffee with 1 cup raspberries and 1 cup white chocolate chips.

ARTISAN FOODS IN THE WEST

Amaltheia Dairy
3880 Penwell Bridge Rd.
Belgrade, MT 59714
(406) 388-5950
www.amaltheiadairy.com

Bozeman Community Food Co-op
908 W. Main St.
Bozeman, MT 59715
(406) 587-4039
www.bozo.coop

Caroline Ranch
Boulder, MT
(406) 225-4280
Manager: Karalee Bancroft
Distributor of SW Montana certified-organic beef, bison, lamb, poultry, and pork.

Cowboy Foods
Bozeman, MT
(800) 759-5489
www.cowboyfoods.com
Barley flours, hull-less barley, hot cereals, barley soup mixes, pancake and bread mixes, barbecue sauce.

Dorothy's
Boise, ID
(800) 657-7449
www.dorothys.cc
Homemade wild huckleberry scone and waffle mixes.

Goods from the Woods
Licking, MO
(800) 267-6680
www.pinenut.com

Harold's Hot Mustard
113 W. Church St.
Absarokee, MT 59001
(406) 328-4385

Henry's Sauce & Condiment Company
405 Stillwater Ave.
Bozeman, MT 59718
(406) 585-3376
www.henryscatsup.com

Huckleberry People
Missoula, MT
(800) 735-6462
www.huckleberrypeople.com
Huckleberry jams, jellies, syrups and toppings, and bread and waffle mixes.

Hearst Ranch Beef
San Francisco, CA
(866) 547-2624
www.hearstranch.com
Grass-fed, hormone-free beef raised on an 80,000-acre coastal ranch; aged steaks shipped overnight.

Jackson Hole Buffalo Meat
Jackson, WY
(800) 543-6328
www.buybuffalomeat.com

Jewel's Flour Shop, Inc.
Livingston, MT
(406) 222-8425
www.jewelsfoods.com

Lava Lake Lamb
Hailey, ID
(208) 788-9778
www.lavalakelamb.com
Certified-organic grass-fed lamb: lamb chops, legs and shanks, racks of lamb, and gourmet sausages.

Meadow Maid Foods
Yoder, WY 82244
(307) 534-2289
www.meadowmaidfoods.com
Gourmet quality 100% grass-fed beef, beef jerky, and vegetables.

Pasta Montana
Great Falls, MT
(406) 761-1516
www.pastamontana.com
Pasta made of superior durum flour; gift baskets.

Planet Natural
Bozeman, MT
(800) 289-6656
www.planetnatural.com
Online natural garden supply, including heirloom herb and flower seeds.

Rollingstone Chèvre
Parma, ID
(208) 722-6460
http://homepage.mac.com/chevre/about.html

Sun Valley Mustard Company
Sun Valley, ID
www.sunvalleymustard.com
Herb-flavored mustards.

Timeless Natural Food
Conrad, MT
(406) 278-5722
www.timelessfood.com
Represents organic family farmers throughout Montana and the surrounding region with new markets for quality crops.

Top of the Hill Meats & Custom Sausages
Polaris, MT
(406) 834-3533
Smoked turkey drumsticks, beef jerky, sausages, bratwurst.

Wilcoxson's Ice Cream
Billings, MT
(406) 259-6572

Wild Bee Honey
Pony, MT
(406) 685-3387

Yakima River Beef
Yakima, WA
(866) 9MY-BEEF
www.feedmysteer.com
Humanely raised, grass-fed Angus beef from a consortium of small family ranches.

ARTISAN CHEF'S TOOLS

Buff Brown
1873 Kimberton Rd.
Phoenixville, PA 19460
(610) 935-2243
www.buffbrown.com
Handmade cutting boards with natural edges.

Mountain Woods
25379 Rye Canyon Rd.
Valencia, CA 91355
(800) 835-0479
www.mountainwoods.com
A California company with a "Made in Montana" section, which includes fiddlebow bread and cheese knives and wooden recipe boxes.

Pequea Valley Forge
Al and Sylvia Stephens
Athens, AL
(256) 729-0758
www.pequeavalleyforge.com
Handforged iron candlesticks, vessels, home hardware, and kitchen tools.

Wood 'N Wares
PO Box 495
Belgrade, MT 59714-0495
(877) 388-6738
Handcrafted wooden spoons, cooking utensils and kitchen tools, spoon oil, and unique food-safe blend of mineral oil and beeswax.

COOKBOOKS AND OTHERS

A Montana Table: Recipes from Chico Hot Springs Resort
Seabring Davis
Globe Pequot Press, 2003
Recipes for many of the fresh and unique creations served throughout the years in the Chico Hot Springs' dining room.
Hardback $22.95
giftshop@chicohotsprings.com

Vintage Restaurant: Handcrafted Cuisine from a Sun Valley Favorite
Jeff Keys
Gibbs Smith, Publisher, 2006
www.gibbs-smith.com

Plenty: One Man, One Woman, and a Raucous Year of Eating Locally
Alisa Smith and James MacKinnon
Crown Publishers, 2007
www.100milediet.org

FOR MORE INFORMATION ON LOCAL SOURCING, SUSTAINABILITY, AND ARTISAN FOODS

Slow Food USA
www.slowfoodusa.org
A nonprofit educational organization dedicated to supporting and celebrating the food traditions of North America. Site maintains lists of local "convivia" and farmers' markets.

Alternative Energy Resources Organization
432 N. Last Chance Gulch
Helena, MT 59601
(406) 443-7272
www.aeromt.org
Producer of "Abundant Montana," a directory of sustainably grown Montana food and guide to Montana's farmers' markets.

Wyoming Farmers Marketing Association
PO Box 20939
Cheyenne, WY 82003
(307) 777-6578
www.wyomingfarmersmarkets.org

Rural Roots, Inc.
Moscow, ID
(208) 883-3462
www.ruralroots.org
Publisher of "Fresh from the Field," Rural Roots' guide to sustainably grown local food.

Western Sustainable Agriculture Research and Education
Utah State University
Logan, UT
(435) 797-2257
wsare.usu.edu

National Sustainable Agriculture Information Service
Fayetteville, AR
(800) 346-9140
www.attra.ncat.org
Online national local food directory.

Eat Wild
(866) 453-8489
www.eatwild.com
Online information about grass-fed beef, lamb, pork, goats, bison, poultry, and dairy products.

FEATURED RESTAURANTS

Brooks Lake Lodge
Dubois, WY
www.brookslake.com
(307) 455-2121

The Bunnery Bakery and Restaurant
Jackson, WY
www.bunnery.com
(307) 734-0075

Chico Hot Springs Resort and Day Spa
Pray, MT
www.chicohotsprings.com
(800) 468-9232

CK's Real Food
Hailey, ID
(208) 778-1223

Log Cabin Café
Silver Gate, MT
(406) 838-2367

Log Haven Restaurant
Salt Lake City, UT
www.log-haven.com
(801) 272-8255

Papoose Creek Lodge
Cameron, MT
www.papoosecreek.com
(888) 674-3030

The Park Café and Grocery
St. Mary, MT
www.parkcafe.us
(406) 732-4482

Pearl Café and Bakery
Missoula, MT
www.pearlcafeandbakery.com
(406) 541-0231

Pine Creek Café
Livingston, MT
(406) 222-3628

Snake Creek Grill
Heber, UT
www.snakecreekgrill.com
(435) 654-2133

Sweetwater Restaurant
Jackson, WY
(307) 733-3553

Vintage Restaurant
Ketchum, ID
(208) 726-9595

Willow Creek Café and Saloon
Willow Creek, MT
(406) 285-3698

Yesterday's Calf-A
Dell, MT
(406) 276-3308

Metric Conversion Chart

Liquid and Dry Measures

U.S.	Canadian	Australian
¼ teaspoon	1 mL	1 ml
½ teaspoon	2 mL	2 ml
1 teaspoon	5 mL	5 ml
1 tablespoon	15 mL	20 ml
¼ cup	50 mL	60 ml
⅓ cup	75 mL	80 ml
½ cup	125 mL	125 ml
⅔ cup	150 mL	170 ml
¾ cup	175 mL	190 ml
1 cup	250 mL	250 ml
1 quart	1 liter	1 litre

Temperature Conversion Chart

Fahrenheit	Celsius
250	120
275	140
300	150
325	160
350	180
375	190
400	200
425	220
450	230
475	240
500	260